Sunshine
in Korea

The South Korean Debate over Policies Toward North Korea

Norman D. Levin and Yong-Sup Han

Supported by the Smith Richardson Foundation

RAND
Center for Asia Pacific Policy

The research described in this report was conducted in RAND's National Security Research Division by the Center for Asia Pacific Policy (CAPP).

Library of Congress Cataloging-in-Publication Data

Levin, Norman D.
    Sunshine in Korea : the South Korean debate over policies toward North Korea / Norman D. Levin, Yong-Sup Han.
        p. cm.
    "MR-1555."
    ISBN 0-8330-3321-2 (pbk.)
    1. Korea (South)—Politics and government—1988– 2. Korea (South)—Foreign relations—Korea (North) 3. Korea (North)—Foreign relations—Korea (South) 4. Kim, Dae Jung, 1925– 5. Korean reunification question (1945–   ) I. Han, Yong-Sup. II. Title.

DS922.4635 .L48 2002
951.904'3—dc21

                                                            2002154385

Cover: Photograph of Mt. Wolchulsan
Copyright: Korea National Tourism Organization

RAND is a nonprofit institution that helps improve policy and decisionmaking through research and analysis. RAND® is a registered trademark. RAND's publications do not necessarily reflect the opinions or policies of its research sponsors.

Cover design by Maritta Tapanainen

Published 2002 by RAND
1700 Main Street, P.O. Box 2138, Santa Monica, CA 90407-2138
1200 South Hayes Street, Arlington, VA 22202-5050
201 North Craig Street, Suite 202, Pittsburgh, PA 15213-1516
RAND URL: http://www.rand.org/
To order RAND documents or to obtain additional information, contact Distribution Services: Telephone: (310) 451-7002;
Fax: (310) 451-6915; Email: order@rand.org

This report examines the public South Korean debate over dealings with North Korea. The focus is on the period since February 1998, when Kim Dae Jung became president of South Korea, and on the major actors, interests, and goals influencing South Korean policies. The report seeks to better understand the sources of controversy over these policies and assess their likely future implications.

Two previous reports provided interim findings. The first, entitled *The South Korean Debate over Policies toward North Korea: Issues and Implications* (MR-1555.0, RAND, 2002), focused on the *content* of the debate over South Korea's new engagement policy—the so-called "sunshine" policy—toward North Korea. The second, entitled *The South Korean Debate over Policies Toward North Korea: Internal Dynamics* (MR-1555.0/1-CAPP, RAND, 2002), focused on the debate's *internal dynamics*—the major actors involved in the debate and their roles in shaping its evolution. This final report updates and integrates the findings of the first two reports and assesses their implications. Findings are current as of October 2002. The report should be of interest to both government officials and specialists on Korea, as well as to general readers interested in Asia and contemporary foreign policy issues.

This research project was conducted under the auspices of the RAND Center for Asia Pacific Policy (CAPP), which aims to improve public policy by providing decisionmakers and the public with rigorous, objective research on critical policy issues affecting Asia and U.S.-Asia relations. CAPP is part of RAND's National Security Research

Division (NSRD). NSRD conducts research and analysis for a broad range of clients including the U.S. Department of Defense, the intelligence community, allied foreign governments, and foundations.

CONTENTS

FIGURE

TABLE

The debate in South Korea over the government's engagement policy toward North Korea (the so-called "sunshine" policy) did not start with Pyongyang's recent admission that it has been secretly pursuing a nuclear weapons program in violation of multiple international commitments. But the evolution of the debate will be an important determinant of how the South Korean and broader international response to this latest North Korean challenge ultimately ends. This report provides a framework for viewing South Korean responses to this challenge. It examines the South Korean debate over policies toward the North, analyzes the sources of controversy, and assesses the debate's implications for South Korea and the United States.

The report finds that much of the public debate is a product of differences among South Koreans over the changes Kim Dae Jung made in South Korea's long existing policy after becoming president in 1998, rather than over the need for some kind of engagement with North Korea per se. While partisan politics are a component of the debate, at its core are some big questions:

- What should be the aim of any effort to achieve greater association with North Korea—"reconciliation" on the basis of Korea being "one people" or "unification" by extending South Korea's democratic, free-market system to the North?

- What role should reciprocity play in this effort?

- What should be the nature and scale of South Korean assistance to North Korea?

- How should political efforts to engage North Korea be balanced against South Korea's security and other important interests?

- How should the effectiveness of the government's policies be evaluated?

What has made the debate so intense is the way in which it has re-opened deeper, long-standing fissures within South Korean society. These fissures divide South Koreans sharply along political, regional, and ideological lines. The latter in particular have contributed to polarizing the debate and undermining public consensus behind the government's policies. In the process, they have made the sunshine policy the core issue in a larger political and ideological struggle.

Although actions by North Korea, and in certain ways the United States, have had important effects, the course of the debate has been heavily shaped by South Korea's own *internal* dynamics. Key factors include the following:

- *The government's minority status:* Rather than try to broaden his base of support in an effort to build greater consensus behind his policies, President Kim generally used his sunshine policy to im-prove his personal political position and party's electoral prospects. While neither unique for a politician nor unreason-able given the president's particular situation, this tendency helped rile the political opposition, politicize what had generally been considered a nonpartisan issue, and exacerbate the task of gaining legislative approval for government policies.

- *The role of reciprocity:* Support for government policies in any democratic society hinges ultimately on a public view that such policies are effective in advancing important national interests. Absent clear manifestations of North Korean reciprocity, and in the context of continued North Korean military provocations, the "payback" for South Korea's largesse became increasingly hard to demonstrate. Among other effects was an administration ten-dency to oversell its policy successes, which over time corroded its credibility.

- *The approach to domestic critics*: The president's confidence and conviction were valuable in providing a compass that kept policy focused despite many challenges. The downside was a certain hardheadedness that closed the policymaking process to all but the closest of the president's aids and blinded the administration to the dangers of mounting domestic opposition. Harsh criticism of those South Koreans who expressed doubts about the government's policy alienated many more in the middle of the political spectrum and narrowed the potential base for national consensus, while it validated long-standing suspicions among South Korean conservatives about the president's ideological propensities and intentions.

- *The war with the press*: Whatever its intentions, the administration's attack on the media under the rubric of "reforming" the press alienated the mainstream media and stimulated a de facto alliance between them and the opposition parties to prevent the government from achieving its objectives. It also exacerbated the administration's difficulty in mobilizing public support for the steps it wanted to take with North Korea, since it could enlist only the leftist media in efforts to rally support for its policies.

- *The lack of trust and willingness to compromise*: These cultural characteristics historically bedeviling Korean politics contributed among other things to political rigidity and a "winner takes all" orientation. This affected the political dynamics at virtually all levels.

Other internal factors contributing to the evolution of events include the extreme personalization of policy, the reluctance to acknowledge the underlying continuity in South Korean policies, and the refusal to convey the actual state of the North-South relationship to the public. The administration's emphasis on "trusting" the North in the absence of a widely apparent basis for this trust, and its periodic efforts to palliate the North through policy and personnel changes, also played a role by creating an impression of governmental naiveté and weakness.

Ultimately, however, the story of how consensus evaporated so quickly is less about particular governmental "mistakes" than about the broader interactions among politicians, press, and public opinion, with civic groups on both sides of an increasingly polarized citizenry serving as flag bearers in a larger political and ideological struggle. This struggle reflects both the continued hold of old, unresolved issues and the impact of South Korea's new process of democratization.

The bad news for government supporters is that the sunshine policy has been dealt a seemingly fatal blow. Even before the revelations concerning North Korea's clandestine uranium enrichment effort, the policy was wrapped up in ideological, regional, and partisan bickering, and the obstacles to unwrapping the policy were substantial. North Korea's startling admission strengthened these obstacles in three ways: It stimulated widespread confusion about North Korean motives; it strengthened those who had long argued that the regime cannot be trusted; and it further undermined public confidence in the administration's handling of North-South relations. As a practical political matter, moreover, the admission preempted all other issues on the policy agenda, while shattering what little was left of Pyongyang's credibility as a negotiating partner. Until and unless the nuclear issue is resolved, the sun is not likely to shine again on North Korea.

Even in the unlikely event that the nuclear issue were resolved quickly, it would be very difficult for the administration to move far forward in inter-Korean relations. Indeed, it would be hard for any government to pursue an effective engagement policy today. Any such policy requires a strong national consensus. Achieving such a consensus, in turn, requires many things: a favorable international environment, a responsive North Korean partner, a perceived balance between South Korean initiatives and North Korean reciprocity, a supportive economy, and public trust. None of these exist today.

In the short term, therefore, advances in North-South relations will be put on ice. The administration will try to maintain the basic framework of its policies—emphasizing continued humanitarian assistance and direct North-South contact—while the nuclear issue is adjudicated. It also will try to preserve the 1994 U.S.–North Korean "Agreed Framework," which froze Pyongyang's overt nuclear program, and as many of the existing North-South agreements as possible. But the task of building a new approach toward inter-Korean relations will fall to President Kim's successor. Overt efforts by North Korea to influence the outcome of the presidential election in December would have an explosive effect inside South Korea.

Apart from the nuclear issue, the internal dynamics of the debate over the sunshine policy suggest several short-term implications:

1. South Korea will continue to be weighed down by history. The intensity of feelings toward President Kim alone will keep the country mired in the past, as will recriminations and debate over his legacy. This could impede timely South Korean responses to international terrorism and other "new era" issues.

2. The political situation is likely to get worse before it gets better. Because of the high stakes, nearly everything the administration does in its remaining months will be geared to winning the election, while the political opposition will do everything it can to besmirch the government's image. Since historically the key to winning elections in South Korea has been to find ways to split the opposition, politics are likely to be nasty.

3. The tendency some South Koreans have to blame the United States for particular problems will likely persist, if not increase further. This is particularly true of Kim Dae Jung's political supporters, whose close personal identification with President Kim almost necessitates a search for scapegoats in the event of policy disappointments. A major downturn in North-South relations will likely be added to the laundry list of issues these groups hold against the United States—a development North Korea may have anticipated in openly acknowledging its clandestine nuclear weapons program but, in any event, one it is certain to actively exploit to inflame tensions inside South Korea and drive a wedge between South Korea and the United States.

Over the long term, the implications of the South Korean public debate are more encouraging. Put simply, democratization is working. Civilian government is permanently in place. The military has been returned to the barracks. And influential institutions—the press, the National Assembly, academia, church and civic organizations—have taken root to inform public policy and check the arbitrary use of executive power. While the position of president continues to weigh heavily in South Korean politics and policy, the highly educated, middle-class electorate has become a real factor affecting his or her prospects for success. As a result, public opinion now matters. The public debate over policy toward the North in this sense is healthy. It brings long-suppressed issues out into the open and allows the sharply divergent views and approaches of South Korean citizens to be aired and adjudicated. Greater consensus—and a broader, steadier center—will undoubtedly emerge over time. The long-term prospect, therefore, is for South Korea to become a more stable and secure democracy.

Getting from here to there, however, will itself take time. Whatever the outcome of the elections in December 2002, the next period will constitute a transition from the era of "the three Kims" (Kim Dae Jung, Kim Young Sam, and Kim Jong-pil) to a new era in South Korean politics. In any such transition period, the fundamental fault lines in society—especially ideological divisions rooted in long-standing, unresolved historical issues—cannot be expected to end overnight. South Korea is no exception. Even a sweeping opposition party (GNP) victory will not end these underlying divisions. This means that for some time to come South Korean politics will remain polarized, personalized, and raw.

The likely effects of the election on policies toward the North are more uncertain. Contrary to the conventional wisdom suggesting that basic South Korean policies will continue no matter who wins the election, the last decade demonstrates that leadership makes a difference. If the GNP wins the election, it is likely that South Korea will adopt a significantly tougher stance toward North Korea. This would entail greater emphasis on reciprocity, verifiable threat reduction, and South Korea's alliance with the United States. It also would involve renewed stress on South Korea's traditional approach toward unification. This would focus more on "peaceful coexistence" than on "reconciliation" as the operative goal of South Korea's policy and give higher priority to strengthening South Korean military and economic capability as the means for achieving its long-term goal of unification on South Korean terms. A GNP government would probably seek to maintain some kind of engagement with North Korea, but it is likely to give greater emphasis to South Korea's security interests as it pursues resolution of the nuclear issue and any resumed North-South dialogue.

If the ruling party (MDP) or some successor party wins, the government would likely maintain the essence of the sunshine policy. Although some effort may be made to distance the new president personally from his predecessor, an MDP government would probably continue to seek inter-Korean "reconciliation." It would also try to protect North-South political interactions by emphasizing the need to resolve the nuclear issue "peacefully through dialogue." An MDP government led by its current leader Roh Moo Hyun might even try to facilitate resolution of the nuclear issue by offering North Korea increased economic assistance or other inducements. Such efforts could increase strains between South Korea and the United States, particularly in the new administration's early, "learning curve" period. Even a Roh Moo Hyun government, however, would have to adapt its stance to the new reality caused by North Korea's defiant acknowledgment of continuing efforts to develop weapons of mass destruction (WMD). Implementation of the North-South denuclearization agreements and North Korea's other international nonnuclear commitments would likely remain a key South Korean demand and impediment to expanded North-South relations.

Whatever the outcome of the elections, the South Korean debate over policies toward the North will present the United States with both a challenge and opportunity. On the one hand, few South Koreans are ready to trade engagement for confrontation. Even fewer want war. This fear of war transcends both party affiliation and ideological predisposition. While critics of the sunshine policy want to see significant changes in South Korea's approach toward the North, most also want to see continued progress toward tension reduction and peaceful coexistence. Avoiding the danger of being seen as an obstacle to peaceful coexistence between the two Koreas, while resolving the WMD issue and pursuing its larger strategic interests, will be a major challenge for U.S. policy.

On the other hand, most South Koreans have lost patience with North Korea. While they tend to see North Korea's actions primarily as defensive measures to ensure its own survival, they recognize such actions as genuine threats to South Korean security. Many also share the view that such continuing bad behavior should not be rewarded. North Korea's admission of an ongoing WMD program exposed its mendacity and malevolence and reinforced the arguments of sunshine policy opponents that all agreements with Pyongyang must be verifiable and reciprocal. This admission also gave greater credence to the long-standing distrust expressed by U.S. officials. As the United States pursues resolution of the nuclear and other outstanding issues with North Korea, it has the opportunity to help establish a basis for greater consensus within South Korea on an appropriate "post-sunshine" policy toward North Korea and greater harmony in U.S. and South Korean approaches.

ACKNOWLEDGMENTS

We are grateful to the many South Koreans within and outside the government who shared their views with us in extensive interviews over three separate field trips. Their candor and insights immeasurably improved our understanding of both the key issues in the South Korean debate and the larger political context in which this debate is being conducted. Although we were unable to name them for purposes of anonymity, they will recognize their contributions in the pages that follow.

We are also grateful to those officials serving in the Clinton and Bush administrations who generously gave their time to share their own perspectives. We hope they too, also necessarily unnamed, will see the multiple ways in which we benefited from these opportunities.

Finally, we want to express our appreciation to several RAND colleagues. Rachel Swanger, former acting director of RAND's Center for Asia-Pacific Policy (CAPP), provided critical support at literally every phase in this research project. Together with her careful review of the draft reports, her creativity and tireless assistance facilitated the research process and significantly improved the final products. Nina Hachigian, CAPP's current director, sustained this support and worked hard to enable the timely dissemination of our research findings. Also, Bruce Bennett provided thoughtful, comprehensive reviews of the draft reports that helped us sharpen our analysis and minimize potential misunderstandings.

While indebted to all these individuals, we alone are responsible for the analysis in this report, as well as for any errors of fact or interpretation.

We also want to express our gratitude to the Smith Richardson Foundation, whose financial support made this project possible. RAND's Center for Asia-Pacific Policy provided important supplementary funding, for which we are very grateful.

Chapter One

INTRODUCTION

In December 2002, South Koreans will elect a new president. The election will be rich in symbolism. Kim Dae Jung, the first leader of South Korea's political opposition ever to be elected president, will himself hand over power. President Kim's departure will mark the end of the decades-long dominance of South Korean politics by the "three Kims"—Kim Dae Jung, Kim Young Sam, and Kim Jong-pil— and herald the gradual emergence of a new, younger generation of leadership that will increasingly shape the country's future. And, while it is not certain at this time which party and candidate will win the election, it *is* certain that the military will not determine the outcome. Such signs of change and continuing movement away from the country's authoritarian past highlight the need for greater analytical attention to the evolution of politics, policies, and trends inside South Korea.

Nowhere is this truer than concerning the government's handling of relations with North Korea. In the last few years, public debate over the administration's "sunshine" policy toward the North has divided South Koreans sharply along political, ideological, and regional lines. In the process, it has uncovered long-standing, underlying fissures within the South Korean body politic, with policy toward the North becoming the core issue in a larger political and ideological struggle. Indeed, the sharp polarization in South Korean society today raises questions about the government's ability to maintain consensus behind any of its policies—including those toward North Korea (DPRK—Democratic People's Republic of Korea). Such questions are particularly acute in the context of North Korea's admission in October 2002 that it is pursuing a secret nuclear weapons program—

an effort that violates the "Nuclear Non-proliferation Treaty" (NPT), the 1994 U.S.-DPRK "Agreed Framework," and the "Joint North-South Declaration on the Denuclearization of the Korean Peninsula."

However these questions are answered, the South Korean debate over policies toward the North and evolution of North-South relations will be major drivers of Korea's future and help determine security prospects throughout the region. This debate and evolution have already raised a number of issues that reinforce latent divisions between the United States and South Korea (ROK—Republic of Korea) and exacerbate the task of managing U.S.-ROK security relations.

This report examines the public debate over the ROK government's policies and the political dynamics that have shaped its evolution. At its heart are three basic questions: What is the debate all about? What accounts for the way it has developed? And what does this imply for the future?

In addressing these questions, the report intends to neither praise nor criticize the Kim Dae Jung administration's policies and/or procedures. A substantial literature already exists emphasizing the administration's accomplishments. An at least equally substantial literature exists itemizing the administration's failures or shortcomings. This report seeks to avoid entanglement in this particular aspect of the debate. Instead, its aim is simply to better understand the sources of controversy over the government's approach toward North Korea and what their implications might be for South Korea and the United States.

The organization of the report reflects such an effort. Chapter Two reviews the relevant historical background, focusing on the evolution of "engagement" as the goal of South Korean policy toward the North and the nature of public debate inside South Korea as this goal was evolving. Chapter Three examines the critical assumptions and central concepts motivating the new policy adopted by President Kim after his inauguration. Chapter Four analyzes the key issues in the public debate over this new policy and the major fault lines in South Korean society underlying, and propelling, public controversy. Chapter Five identifies the major actors and describes their respective positions on the government's approach to North Korea. Chapter Six explores the process by which the views and actions of all these actors affected public debate over government policy. Chapter Seven concludes by assessing the sources of public controversy existing today, the likely short-term effects on South Korean policy, and the potential longer-term implications for South Korea, the United States, and U.S.-ROK relations.

Chapter Two

THE HISTORICAL SETTING

THE EVOLUTION OF ENGAGEMENT

On October 13, 2000, the Norwegian Nobel Committee awarded that year's Nobel Peace Prize to South Korea's president, Kim Dae Jung—the first time in history that a Korean had been selected for this prestigious award.[1] In explaining its decision, the committee praised the president for his efforts over the decades "for democracy and human rights in South Korea and East Asia in general." But the committee stressed the president's work "for peace and reconciliation with North Korea in particular," lauding his "sunshine" policy of engagement with North Korea for reducing tension between the two Koreas and creating hope that the Cold War in Korea too will soon come to an end. The Nobel Committee's decision may have reinforced an impression overseas that South Korean efforts to draw North Korea out of its self-imposed isolation and engage it in steps toward reducing tension on the Korean Peninsula began only in February 1998 with the inauguration of Kim Dae Jung.

This impression, to a certain extent, is understandable. For more than two decades after its establishment in 1948, the ROK denied the very existence of North Korea. Insisting that it alone was the legitimate government on the Korean Peninsula, successive governments focused their efforts on preventing international recognition of the DPRK. Even after they dropped these efforts, ROK governments

---

[1]The formal press release announcing the award can be found at www.nobel.se/peace/laureates/2000/press.html, the official web site of the Nobel Foundation.

continued to place primary emphasis on developing the South Korean economy, rather than on interacting with Pyongyang, so as to create the wherewithal to ultimately achieve "victory" over the regime in North Korea. South Korean leaders also continued to denounce North Korea's Communist system, while placing priority on countering actual and potential North Korean acts of aggression. The consistency and single-mindedness with which Kim Dae Jung has pursued engagement with the North as president himself reinforces the contrast with most of his predecessors.

The personalization of "engagement" with Kim Dae Jung, however, is misleading. In fact, South Korea's engagement policy evolved both incrementally and over a long period of time. While detailing this evolution is beyond this report's purview, the major milestones might be highlighted since they bear directly on the current debate over the government's policies.[2]

Former South Korean President Park Chung Hee took the first, fledging steps toward some form of engagement. In his August 15, 1970 speech commemorating the 25th anniversary of Korea's liberation from Japanese colonial rule, Park suggested for the first time that the ROK was willing to coexist peacefully with Pyongyang and urged the North to replace the hostile military confrontation with socioeconomic competition.[3] The historic July 4, 1972, North-South Joint Communiqué, which followed months of both private-level (Red Cross) talks and secret official contacts between the two governments, codified this policy departure. With its emphasis on pursuing unification independently, peacefully, and based on national unity transcending the differences between the two systems, the joint

---

[2] For more detailed accounts of the historical evolution, see: Hakjoon Kim, *Unification Policies of South and North Korea* (Seoul National University Press, 1978); Hakjoon Kim, "The Development of the Unification Debates in South and North Korea: From a South Korean Nationalism Perspective," in Gun Ho Song and Man Kil Kang, eds., *Korean Nationalism, Vol. I* (Seoul: Changjakgwa Bipyungsa, 1982); Jong-Chun Baek, *Probe for Korean Reunification* (Research Center for Peace and Unification of Korea, 1988); Jinwook Choi and Sun-Song Park, *The Making of a Unified Korea—Policies, Positions, and Proposals* (Korea Institute for National Unification, 1997); and Yu-hwan Koh, "Unification Policies of Two Koreas and Outlook for Unity," *Korea Focus*, Vol. 8, No. 6, Nov.–Dec. 2000.

[3] A text, entitled "President Park's 'August 15 Declaration,'" is available online at www.unikorea.go.kr.

communiqué concretized the ROK's new willingness to engage in direct interactions with the North as part of its de facto acceptance of peaceful coexistence.[4] Park's "Special Foreign Policy Statement Regarding Peace and Unification" the following year (June 23, 1973) enshrined this willingness further by dropping South Korea's historic opposition to Pyongyang's participation in international organizations and to the simultaneous entry of both Koreas into the United Nations.[5]

Park's successor, Chun Doo Hwan, went one step further. In his 1982 "New Year Policy Statement" announcing a "new peaceful unification formula" for South Korea, Chun urged that the "unnatural relations" between the two Koreas be brought to an end and be replaced by "normal contacts that promote the national well-being."[6] These contacts should be based on fully "normalized relations," he said, and should promote a broad range of North-South exchanges and cooperation, including in trade, transportation, communications, and many other areas. Repeating an idea he had raised the previous year, Chun formally proposed the exchange of high-level delegations to work out procedures for a summit meeting between the top leaders of the two Koreas that would serve as the impetus for a normalization of relations.

The approach of Roh Tae Woo, who succeeded Chun as South Korea's president, represents a significant extension of this evolving policy. Underlying his government's approach was both a novel analysis of the reasons for Korea's continued division and a new image of North Korea. This was expressed in a "Special Presidential Declaration" in July 1988.[7] In this declaration, Roh linked Korea's continued division not to the nature of the North Korean system and the aggressive policies pursued by its leaders, as had most previous governments, but rather to the fact that "both the south and the north have been regarding the other as an adversary." Accordingly,

---

[4]For the text of the joint communiqué, see *Peace and Cooperation—White Paper on Korean Unification 1996* (ROK Ministry of National Unification, 1996), pp. 183–185.

[5]An online text is available at www.unikorea.go.kr.

[6]"President Chun's Declaration of 'The Formula for National Reconciliation and Democratic Unification,'" January 22, 1982, ibid.

[7]"Special Presidential Declaration for National Self-Esteem, Unification, and Prosperity," July 4, 1988, ibid.

he argued, South Korea needed to think of North-South relations more as a potential partnership in the pursuit of common prosperity.

Based on this notion, Roh proposed mutual exchanges, open trade, and North-South international cooperation to develop a "joint national community" in which both Koreas could prosper. He gave substance to this proposal by developing much of the legal and administrative machinery for regulating North-South economic interactions, including the establishment of an Inter-Korean Exchange and Cooperation Promotion Committee to oversee exchanges between the two Koreas. Roh also planted two seeds in the July 1988 declaration that would later blossom as key components of South Korean policy. One was his call for the "balanced development" of the economies in the two Koreas. In the context of North Korea's economic crisis and South Korea's mounting economic superiority, this implied potential ROK economic assistance to Pyongyang. The other was his indication of South Korean willingness to not only countenance but also actively facilitate the improvement of North Korean relations with the West, particularly the United States and Japan.

Roh subsequently added his own call for a North-South summit meeting to that of his predecessor, folding all these initiatives into a larger South Korean effort to build a "national commonwealth" that would provide a prolonged period of peace on the road to unification.[8] This notion of a "national commonwealth" corresponds to the interim phase of the Roh government's gradual, three-stage unification formula, a phase involving the formalization of a range of activities typically carried out by sovereign states under the rubric of "peaceful coexistence." As such, it does not imply any formal political integration. Rather, the government's intent was simply to communicate to Pyongyang South Korea's desire to find a way to live together peacefully. But the "commonwealth" idea does suggest a willingness to live with the North—and a degree of inter-Korean cooperation and exchange—which constituted a significant extension of existing policy.

---

[8]The broad approach was spelled out at greatest length in "President Roh Tae Woo's Special Address for the Korean National Community Unification Formula," September 11, 1989, ibid.

The landmark "Agreement on Reconciliation, Non-Aggression, and Exchanges and Cooperation between the South and the North" signed in December 1991—often called the "Basic Agreement"— capped the ROK's long-standing efforts to encourage Pyongyang to accept some form of peaceful coexistence. This agreement constitutes one of the most significant documents in the history of inter-Korean relations. It committed the two sides to respect each other's political systems and to never use force or threaten military action. It called for the active promotion of inter-Korean cooperation, exchange, and travel. And it established an intricate web of committees and subcommittees to implement the agreed-upon measures. Together with the range of related high-level exchanges and agreements (such as the Joint Declaration on the De-Nuclearization of the Korean Peninsula) in the early 1990s, the Basic Agreement concretized South Korea's commitment to engagement with the North and to facilitating Pyongyang's opening to the international community.[9]

The succeeding administration of Kim Young Sam adhered to the key components of Roh's policy, despite some wavering in the policy's implementation.[10] Indeed, it reinforced Roh's policy by publicly professing no desire for either "unification by absorption"—the code words for German-style unification based on the collapse of the Communist system—or seeing "the North isolated from the rest of the world."[11] Echoing his predecessor's stress on the need to promote "coexistence and co-prosperity," President Kim reaffirmed the goal of a gradual, long-term, peaceful process of unification, with the building of a single "national community" being the interim objective. He also reiterated South Korea's previous calls for a summit meeting to stimulate North-South reconciliation, which North Korean leader Kim Il Sung formally accepted in June 1994. Had the lat-

---

[9]For texts of both the Basic Agreement and the Joint Declaration, see *Peace and Cooperation—White Paper on Korean Unification 1996,* op. cit., pp. 200–209.

[10]For one of the more sympathetic accounts of Kim's widely criticized "inconsistency," see Yongho Kim, "Inconsistency or Flexibility? The Kim Young Sam Government's North Korea Policy and Its Domestic Variants," *International Journal of Korean Unification Studies,* Vol. 8, 1999 (The Korea Institute for National Unification, December 1999), pp. 225–245.

[11]See, for example, "President Kim Young Sam's 1994 Liberation Day Speech," August 15, 1994, at www.unikorea.go.kr.

ter's sudden death in July not occurred just days before the scheduled summit, which led to its indefinite postponement, the Nobel
Peace Prize might well have gone to a different Kim.

To be sure, Kim Young Sam made clear, as had all of his predecessors, that the quest for unification could only be "centered on the
values of freedom and democracy."[12] But he also shared Roh Tae
Woo's commitment to encouraging North Korea to set aside their
ideological rivalry and, as he said in his August 1994 Liberation Day
speech, engaging Pyongyang in steps toward building "a national
community within which all Koreans can live together." He further
proposed "Four Party Talks" among the United States, China, and
the two Koreas, primarily as a means for bringing Pyongyang into
discussions with South Korea.[13] Insisting that the "problems of the
North are our own problems" as well, Kim backed up this talk by do-
nating 150,000 tons of rice to relieve Pyongyang's severe food shortage—the first time South Korea had ever provided the North direct
assistance.

This brief review suggests something of the evolutionary quality of
South Korea's engagement policy. The incremental nature of the
evolution provided many precedents for, and a foundation on which
to build, future policy. Among engagement's many wellsprings were
several growing South Korean convictions:

- *Deterrence alone is not enough:* As the Cold War structure of international politics first moved to détente and then collapsed
  altogether, ROK leaders saw a need for greater flexibility in their
  approach toward Pyongyang. With South Korea's dramatic economic success and inexorable shift in the balance of power be-

---

[12]While Roh Tae Woo placed notable stress on the need to "restore national homo-
geneity" without regard to "differing ideologies and political systems," even he was
careful to insist that "a democratic nation that guarantees the human rights of every
individual . . . is the only choice for a unified Korea." See, for example, "President Roh
Tae Woo's Special Address," op. cit.

[13]Kim's emphasis on the need for engagement was also reflected in his decision to
authorize the United States to deal directly with North Korea on nuclear issues following Pyongyang's withdrawal from the nuclear Non-Proliferation Treaty in March 1993.
Although this contrasted sharply with previous ROK opposition to direct U.S.-DPRK
dealings in which it was not a participant, "it was important," as Kim's foreign minister, Han Sung-Joo, later put it, "to engage North Korea in any way possible." Sung-Joo
Han, "The Koreas' New Century," *Survival*, Vol. 42, No. 4, Winter 2000–01, p. 85.

tween the two Koreas, South Koreans saw an opportunity to advance both their short-term goal of reducing tensions and long-term interest in facilitating unification essentially on South Korean terms. North Korea's escalating economic crisis in the 1990s bolstered these incentives by creating the prospect of a messy North Korean implosion. One consequence was a growing tendency in the South Korean public to regard North Korea more as a lifestyle threat—in the sense of South Korea being overwhelmed by refugees or having to bear the astronomical costs of unification—than as an imminent security danger. Together with the dramatic process of democratization that occurred almost simultaneously in the ROK, such developments reinforced the view in the government and public alike that deterrence—while indispensable—needed to be supplemented by some form of engagement. South Korean awareness of the potential costs of miscalculation and conflict, strengthened significantly by North Korea's effort to develop weapons of mass destruction and increasing international isolation, further reinforced this view by creating a general sense that major efforts are needed to ensure war is avoided.[14]

- *Efforts to engage North Korea should include significant economic and humanitarian components:* In the period leading up to the Kim Dae Jung administration, no South Korean leader treated the threat from the North lightly. Each identified the absence of change in North Korean domestic and foreign policies as the principal obstacle to peaceful unification. And all made clear that major steps by Seoul hinged on North Korean willingness to end its hostile actions, accept the ROK as a legitimate negotiating partner, and take concrete steps to reduce military tensions on the peninsula. Alongside this emphasis, however, successive South Korean governments increasingly came to identify the high level of mutual distrust as a key obstacle to reducing ten-

---

[14]The repeated U.S. articulation of this theme in the mid-1990s and emphasis on the need to supplement deterrence with a broader strategy for managing the growing risks associated with North Korea's evolving situation undoubtedly contributed to the emerging South Korean consensus. See, for example, the speech by then U.S. Ambassador to South Korea James Laney, "What Are We Going to Do About North Korea?" Address to the Conference on the International Economic Implications of Unification, Seoul, Korea, June 28, 1996.

sions. They also came to see the primitive economic conditions in the North and yawning social gap between the two peoples as major impediments to the ultimate integration of the two systems. Building trust gradually through economic and humanitarian exchanges thus came to be seen as a means for advancing both short- and long-term South Korean interests.

- *A summit is essential:* The emphasis successive South Korean governments gave to a summit meeting between the top leaders of the two Koreas reflects several shared considerations. One had to do with the extreme nature of totalitarianism in North Korea. Since virtually all important matters are decided by the "Great Leader" himself, South Korean leaders believed that nothing could be resolved without meeting personally with him and getting his imprimatur on new policies. Another concerned political considerations within South Korea. Given the strong public aspiration for unification and the decades of disparagement South Korean leaders endured from their North Korean counterparts, they saw a summit meeting as a means to strengthen their internal political position while simultaneously raising their external stature. A third consideration related to the distrust alluded to above. Given the depth of mutual suspicion, South Korean leaders came to feel that only by sitting down with their Northern counterparts and establishing some personal level of trust could a basis be built for expanded interactions between the two countries. A broader cultural tendency among South Koreans to see the North-South conflict more as a result of political than military factors may have reinforced the perceived need for high-level dialogue first before attempting to resolve major substantive bilateral issues. North Korea's lack of interest, until former U.S. President Jimmy Carter's intervention during the nuclear crisis in 1994, precluded the holding of such a summit meeting. But it was a strong and widely shared goal of South Korean leaders for nearly two decades.

Together with the "lessons" South Koreans increasingly drew from Germany's experience about the high cost of even peaceful unification, these growing convictions underpinned efforts to engage North Korea in the period prior to the Kim Dae Jung administration. They bolstered advocates of Kim's sunshine policy as well and provided fertile soil for the new president's own engagement aspirations. The notable efforts by previous administrations to sound out Kim's views when he was still a leader of the political opposition and incorporate them in government policy further facilitated these aspirations.[15] Indeed, while there was always opposition in certain quarters to dealing with North Korea, by the time Kim was inaugurated, engaging North Korea had largely moved from a question of "whether" to a matter of "how" and "when."

THE EMERGENCE OF DEBATE

Sharp public debate over the government's policies toward the North was similarly a gradual development. This may be hard to appreciate from the scene today. One foreign observer of South Korean politics captured this well when he wrote, somewhat plaintively, that the "sunshine policy is for statesmen, not politicians."[16] By this he meant that the government's effort to engage North Korea in pursuit of peaceful coexistence requires greater patience and longer time horizons than are manifested in South Korean politics today. A former high-level South Korean official once privately expressed a similar thought. Alluding not to the sunshine policy per se but to the general domestic political turmoil affecting South Korean policies, he sighed and said only half-facetiously: "I used to believe in democracy, but now I'm not so certain." Both of these comments reflect an important reality: Politics in South Korea are here to stay. Like government officials themselves, academics and outside observers can no longer address South Korean policy toward the North purely in its "foreign policy" dimensions.

The fact is, however, that this is a relatively new phenomenon. For much of its history, South Korean politics were largely free of the

---

[15]The efforts of Hong-Koo Lee, Minister of Unification during President Roh's administration and later chairman of the ruling party, prime minister, and ambassador to the United States, were particularly noteworthy. Lee is widely seen as the intellectual father and architect of Roh's "national commonwealth" proposal. As Minister of Unification, he actively consulted with other South Korean leaders, including all three of the major opposition party leaders (Kim Dae Jung, Kim Young Sam, and Kim Jong-pil), and incorporated their views into the administration's new engagement policies.

[16]David I. Steinberg, "The Republic of Korea's Sunshine Policy: Domestic Determinants of Policy and Performance," in Chung-in Moon and David I. Steinberg, eds., *Kim Dae-jung Government and Sunshine Policy: Promises and Challenges* (Yonsei University Press, 1999), p. 57.

kind of rancorous public debate characteristic in the country today. Although there have always been sharply divergent viewpoints, significant public discord was constrained by the Cold War structure of international politics and the objective threat from North Korea. Equally important was a host of purely internal factors, including South Korea's tradition of repressive rule, authoritarian practices, and ideological rigidity. With only a few exceptions, the external and internal environments combined to suppress public debate and dissension.

The basic pattern dates to the period following Korea's "liberation" from Japanese colonial rule in 1945 and the establishment of the Republic of Korea three years later. During this period, South Korea was sharply divided between rightists and leftists over how to respond to the division of the peninsula and the major powers' plan to impose a trusteeship on Korea.[17] Following the establishment of the Republic of Korea in 1948, President Rhee enacted a National Security Law aimed at silencing his leftist opponents, whom he regarded as a threat not only to his rule but to the ROK's very existence. The law inhibited debate on unification issues by banning all "Communist" activities.

The Korean War (1950–1953) cemented the ideological confrontation between the North and South. In the period thereafter, neither side tolerated voices that diverged from the official government position. As protests mounted in the South against President Rhee's dictatorial regime in the mid-1950s, government leaders denounced the protesters for weakening South Korea's national security and forcibly put down the protests.[18] They further restricted freedom of speech in 1958 by amending the already stringent National Security Law to provide death sentences or long prison terms for such ambiguous

---

[17]The "conservatives," led ultimately by Rhee Syngman, came to favor separate elections in the South and the establishment of an independent South Korean government backed by the United States, with unification being a goal to be pursued thereafter. The "progressives," behind leaders like Kim Ku and Kim Kyu Shik, opposed separate elections in the South on the grounds that they would perpetuate the division of the peninsula. Instead, they insisted on unification first followed by the establishment of a unified, neutral Korean government.

[18]Yong Pyo Hong, "State Security and Regime Security (*Kukga Anbo wa Junggwon Anbo*): The Case of President Syngman Rhee's Security Policy 1953–1960," *Journal of Korean Association of International Studies*, Vol. 36, No. 3, 1997, pp. 252–258.

crimes as "disseminating Communist propaganda." This was part of a larger effort to muzzle government critics and uproot elements seen as sympathetic to North Korea.[19] The effort stifled public debate over unification issues until Rhee was overthrown in 1960 by massive student demonstrations.

Debate over the government's policies toward North Korea exploded following Rhee's downfall, fed by radical intellectuals and students bent on social revolution and facilitated by a new permissiveness toward civil freedom. In this brief but heady period, numerous leftist political parties were formed to contend for seats in the National Assembly. Together with other political and civic groups, they sought to bolster "progressive" elements throughout South Korean society. Not surprisingly given their political and ideological coloration, the positions they took on North-South issues were very close to North Korea's position. For example, many called for "unification first, national construction later," "neutralization" of the Korean Peninsula, and "self-reliant unification" without external intervention (code words for the withdrawal of U.S. military forces). Others urged unconditional cooperation with North Korea and active promotion of North-South exchanges, acceptance of North Korean economic assistance, and institution of "democratic socialism" in the South. Motivating these positions were the paramount goals of "peace" and a "grand national [i.e., pan-Korean] solidarity."

North Korea did all it could to rile things further, adroitly promoting anti-Rhee and anti-U.S. sentiment to exacerbate South Korea's growing domestic turmoil. Kim Il Sung proposed the immediate withdrawal of foreign troops from South Korea, for example, and a free election by Koreans without any foreign intervention. He called for a joint meeting attended by representatives of all political parties and social organizations to discuss a unified government. And he professed a willingness to allow free travel and exchange of materials be-

---

[19]One example: In 1958, President Rhee arrested Cho Bong Am, the leader of the opposition Progressive Party because he was irate over the latter's call for "peaceful unification," which challenged the government's official policy of "unification by marching northward." Charging him with espionage and National Security Law violations, Rhee subsequently had him convicted and executed. In 1959, he banned publication of the major opposition newspaper, the *Kyonghyang Sinmun*, in a further attempt to prevent public discussion. See Richard C. Allen, *Korea's Syngman Rhee* (Charles E. Tuttle Company, 1960) for a fuller account.

tween the two Koreas, while urging the formation of a joint inter-Korean economic committee to help South Korea overcome its economic difficulties. North Korea's emphasis on the strength of the North Korean economy and willingness to provide its "brothers and sisters" in the South economic assistance helped fuel a vehement student movement demanding acceptance of such assistance and the initiation of joint meetings with North Korean counterparts.

In response, the new Chang Myon government that replaced Rhee insisted on "first construction, then unification"—which, even packaged as a "new conservatism," did not diverge much from Rhee's approach. It also maintained Rhee's broader anti-Communist policy.[20] Seeing North Korea's proposals as attempts to subvert the South Korean government, the government rejected all of its overtures for exchange and cooperation. This did not halt, however, South Korea's growing turmoil and political disorganization.

The military coup in May 1961 did. Perceiving the domestic unrest as leading South Korea to the brink of collapse, Park Chung Hee, the leader of the coup and South Korea's next president, quickly moved to restore social order by suppressing the unification movement entirely. He also enacted a new, even tougher "anti-Communism" law that designated anti-Communism as national policy and the top goal of the nation. Banning all talk about unification, President Park concentrated national efforts instead on rapid economic construction. The result: South Koreans' aspiration for unification and open debate on inter-Korean issues was iced for another decade.

In the 1970s, some cracks in the ice surfaced. President Park stimulated this process himself. Aware of the public's pent-up desire for unification and more confident about trends in the North-South economic competition, Park initiated a dialogue with North Korea that led to the historic July 4, 1972, North-South Joint Communiqué. As noted above, this codified South Korea's de facto acceptance of North Korea's existence and its willingness to participate in direct interactions. The communiqué and a subsequent series of North-South negotiating sessions opened the door for South Korean officials, academics, institute analysts, and others to begin to explore a

---

[20]Hakjoon Kim, *Korean Matters and International Politics (Hankuk Munje wa Kukje Jungchi)*, (Seoul: Pak Young Sa, 1995), p. 653.

range of issues pertaining to inter-Korean cooperation. South Korean discussions and exploration of gradual, functionalist approaches to unification as a means for facilitating greater North-South integration also date to this period.

These cracks were carefully contained, however. At precisely the same time that Park was opening a dialogue with Pyongyang and moving toward official acceptance of peaceful coexistence, he reinforced his seemingly permanent dictatorship by amending the Constitution to perpetuate his personal rule. Under the guise of the new *Yushin* ("Revitalizing Reform") Constitution, Park banned all political activities and open opposition to his rule. He also promulgated a state of national emergency under which expressed criticism of his regime was equated with efforts to destabilize South Korean society—and hence with support for North Korea's attempt to bring the entire peninsula under its control. These acts, aided by the collapse of South Vietnam and South Korean fears of a U.S. withdrawal from Korea in the mid-1970s, stifled debate over policies regarding North Korea.

Throughout the *Yushin* regime (1972–1979), President Park equated national security with the militarization of South Korea's politics, economy, society, and culture and saw opposition to his North Korea policy as particularly damaging.[21] Opposition groups were accordingly infiltrated, co-opted, or forced underground, with many continuing their activities (despite dwindling numbers) as part of "people's" movement. In this hothouse environment, however, most of these activities centered on efforts to resist the military dictatorship. What passed for public debate tended to focus on issues pertaining to democratization rather than unification.

After a brief flare-up between the assassination of President Park in October 1979 and the formal assumption of power by General Chun Doo Hwan in August 1980, the situation resumed its previous pattern. Chun disbanded all four South Korean political parties

---

[21]Youngnok Koo, "Foreign Policy Decision Making," in Youngnok Koo and Sung-Joo Han, eds., *The Foreign Policy of the Republic of Korea* (New York: Columbia University Press, 1985), pp. 22–44. Also see Youngnok Koo, "South Korea's Security Strategy" (*Hankuk ui Anb o Junryak*), *National Strategy* (*Kukga Junryak*), Spring 1995, Vol. 1, No. 1 (Seoul: Sejong Institute), p. 50.

(although he allowed new parties to be formed a year later under tight restrictions). He banned over 800 people from participating in politics (although roughly a third of them were later allowed to resume their political activities). And he forced the merger of all press, news agencies, and broadcasting companies throughout the country so as to control their reporting (although this was relaxed over time under close government supervision). As part of this extensive political repression, Chun indicted opposition leader Kim Dae Jung for participating in "antistate" activities and fostering "rebellion," subsequently convicting him by military court-martial and sentencing him to death.[22] He also placed a political ban on the other two major opposition leaders, Kim Young Sam and Kim Jong-pil, which was not lifted until 1985. The effect was to muzzle debate over the regime's North Korea policies. In response, "progressive" groups stepped up their underground activities, focused on resisting the harsh repression and increasing public pressures for democratization.

The emphasis on democratization as the focus of opposition activity, however, should not obscure an important development: the gradual creation of a link between the struggle for democracy and the desire for unification. With material conditions improving and the middle class growing, the trade-offs South Koreans had long made to ensure their economic security—prolongation of dictatorial rule and postponement of unification—became both more evident and less tolerable. In this environment, many came to see achieving democracy in South Korea not only as a critical need in its own right but as the essential first step toward promoting peace and unification on the peninsula more broadly. For "progressives" in particular, the struggle to achieve democracy in South Korean society became synonymous with the struggle to promote reconciliation between the two Koreas. After three decades of successive dictatorial regimes, they had come to believe that this latter struggle could never succeed so long as repressive governments ruled South Korea. "Democracy first" thus became the watchword for many opposition groups who

---

[22]Kim's personal "three-stage unification theory" was cited as one of the offenses for which he warranted the death penalty. U.S. pressure secured Kim's release in 1982, although it was three more years before he was allowed to resume his political activities.

saw democratization in South Korea as the "historically destined path" to ultimate unification.[23]

Constraints on public debate finally began to loosen after President Chun, bowing to strong public pressure, agreed in 1987 to new constitutional arrangements allowing direct presidential elections. This led the following year to South Korea's first peaceful transfer of power in its then 40-year history. As described above, Chun's successor, ruling party head and former General Roh Tae Woo, took significant steps to foster peaceful coexistence with North Korea while gradually relaxing political controls in South Korea. The end of the Cold War abroad facilitated this process, as did North Korea's mounting economic desperation. For the first time, South Koreans were becoming confident about both short- and long-term prospects. This gave greater leeway for the expression of diverse opinions.

President Roh himself encouraged this process, even tolerating the open efforts by a prominent South Korean opposition leader to arrange a meeting for himself with North Korean leader Kim Il Sung. Roh also made an effort to incorporate the views of all three major political opposition leaders in his government's three-stage, "commonwealth" approach to unification—an approach that embodies South Korea's formal acceptance of peaceful coexistence and remains official government policy today. Along with Roh's broader push to establish relations with the world's Communist powers, often labeled *Nordpolitik* in a nod to the model West Germany's *Ostpolitik* provided, these initiatives reinforced the sense of growing openness and change and elicited general support from the South Korean public.

Despite this general support, many active duty and retired military officers opposed the government's directions. And conservatives still controlled the policy process. This placed significant constraints on both national policy and public discussions. While low-level debate emerged over such issues, it did not create sharp divisions in South Korean society. The dramatic success of the administration's *Nord-*

---

[23]Keun Il Ryu, "Democratization and Peace" and Hak Kyu Sohn, "Political Change and Peace," in Ho Je Lee, ed., *Peace on the Korean Peninsula* (Seoul: Bobmunsa, 1989), pp. 271–287 and 288–330, respectively.

politik policies and movement toward peaceful coexistence with North Korea—symbolized by the landmark 1991 North-South "Basic Agreement" in particular—also helped constrain debate. Together with the collapse of the Soviet Union and Communist states of Eastern Europe, these policies pulled the rug out from leftist groups that had begun to reemerge in South Korea and to undercut support for radical measures.

Public debate stepped up during the presidency of Kim Young Sam (1993–1997), Roh's successor. Of all South Korea's presidents up to that point, President Kim was the most determined to establish a new era of reconciliation and cooperation with North Korea. Moreover, as a long-time leader of South Korean democratic forces and South Korea's first civilian president after three decades of military-dominated regimes, he could build on the successes of his predecessors without being handicapped by their military backgrounds and political orientations. Unfortunately for him, however, North Korea's decision to withdraw from the nuclear Non-proliferation Treaty one month after President Kim's inauguration precipitated a major crisis on the peninsula. Kim's perceived inconsistency in dealing with North Korea as this crisis evolved over the next year and a half jeopardized his North Korea policy as a whole and stimulated widespread criticism of his management of foreign affairs.

Two additional factors fed public discord. One was U.S. dominance of the dialogue with North Korea to resolve the nuclear crisis. As noted above, President Kim went along with this dominance partly because he had little choice but also because he considered it essential, given the high stakes, to engage North Korea in any way possible.[24] But this decision made the administration vulnerable to charges from the left that it had mortgaged South Korea's policy to the strategic interests of the United States. The other factor was Kim's decision to merge his party with the conservative ruling party of former President Roh in order to secure his election. While successful as an electoral strategy, this decision inherently limited Kim's freedom of action, since he was required to ensure that his government's policies reflected the preferences of his party's conservative mainstream. The collapse of the scheduled inter-Korean summit

[24]Sung-Joo Han, "The Koreas' New Century," op. cit., p. 85.

meeting following Kim Il Sung's sudden death in 1994 opened the administration to sharp criticism by Kim Dae Jung's opposition party, leftist labor unions, and progressive civic groups that the administration was responsible for the ensuing deadlock in North-South relations.

By the end of Kim Young Sam's term, public debate over policies toward North Korea had thus become a notable feature of South Korean politics. The debate's policy significance was limited, however, by continued conservative dominance, weak "progressive" leadership, and a growing public consensus on the need for some kind of engagement with North Korea despite its bellicose behavior. It took the election of Kim Dae Jung—the first time in South Korea's national history that power was transferred peacefully from the ruling to the opposition party—for the public debate to fully blossom. This was partly due to idiosyncratic factors. But it was also due to the fact that the pursuit of engagement under Kim Dae Jung was anything but a simple continuation of previous policy. Indeed, in critical respects it represented a major departure.

Chapter Three

THE SUNSHINE POLICY: PRINCIPLES AND MAIN ACTIVITIES

Kim Dae Jung's personal commitment to engagement was unmistakable. Right after his election he suggested metaphorically that, as in the famous Aesop fable, he would use "sunshine" as a vehicle for persuading North Korea to give up its hostility and end its international isolation. In his inaugural address he emphasized that he would make reconciliation and cooperation with North Korea a top priority of his administration, despite Pyongyang's continuing bellicosity and the severe financial crisis that had just hit South Korea. Thereafter, he ordered that the word "unification" be dropped from all descriptions of his government's policies to the North, substituting instead terms like "constructive engagement policies" to avoid stimulating North Korea's fear of being "absorbed" by its stronger southern brother. Castigating past South Korean governments for their alleged inconsistency and insincerity, administration officials stressed that they would be different in consistently adhering to reconciliation and cooperation whatever temporary difficulties might arise.[1] In the process, President Kim communicated two mega mes-

---

[1]The then-president of the Korea Institute for National Unification (KINU), a governmental organization under the Ministry of National Unification, made this latter point explicit.

> Unlike past governments that pursued the dual goals of reconciliation and cooperation on the surface and a sort of unification by absorption in fact, [he argued,] the current government has expressly ruled out attempts to absorb North Korea in favor of a more positive engagement policy designed to promote peaceful coexistence, reconciliation and cooperation between North and South Korea (Yang Young-shik, "Kim Dae-Jung Admin-

sages: that his administration's goals would be peaceful coexistence, not unification; and that its policies would seek to reassure the North Korean regime of, not undermine confidence in, South Korea's good intentions.[2]

The administration formally predicated its policy on three basic principles: no toleration of North Korean armed provocations, no South Korean efforts to undermine or absorb the North, and active ROK attempts to promote reconciliation and cooperation between the two Koreas.[3] These principles were designed to communicate that, while South Korea would maintain a strong deterrent posture and respond to potential North Korean provocations, it would not seek to provoke the regime's collapse. Rather it would try to foster a range of cooperative bilateral activities and facilitate North Korean interactions with the United States, Japan, and the broader international community.

Although not rising quite to the level of "basic principles," the administration identified two other core policy components. One is the separation of politics and economics. Formally, this meant allowing South Korea's private sector greater leeway in making its own decisions concerning trade and investment with the North and easing restrictions that hindered inter-Korean business, while limiting the government's role primarily to matters of humanitarian and other official assistance. In practice, it meant not holding South Korean economic interactions with the North hostage to good North Korean behavior in other areas.

---

istration's North Korea Policy," *Korea Focus*, November–December 1998, p. 48).

[2]Formally, President Kim has never jettisoned the *long-term* goal of unification. Nor has he presented any new unification formula to take the place of the "national community" approach adopted by Roh Tae Woo. This leaves both of these standing as Korea's official unification policy. And even President Kim's "personal" three-stage unification formula posits peaceful coexistence as only the first stage of a much longer-term process, with the second stage being a confederation and the third being full unification. For all *practical* purposes, however, the goal of his administration's policy has been simply on achieving peaceful coexistence. As his foreign minister put it at the time, "Seoul's constructive engagement policies aim for peaceful coexistence. The longer-term goal of unification can wait." Hong Soon-young, "Thawing Korea's Cold War," *Foreign Affairs*, May/June 1999, p. 10.

[3]"North Korea Policy of the Kim Dae Jung Administration," available online at www.unikorea.go.kr.

In emphasizing the separation of politics and economics, the administration clearly understood the importance of expanded economic exchanges for creating a more peaceful atmosphere on the Korean Peninsula. It also understood North Korea's dire economic situation and greater potential receptivity to economic, rather than political, inducements. Interestingly, however, administration officials explained and rationalized the importance of separating economics and politics more in terms of its effect in fostering change inside North Korea itself. As Kang In-duk, President Kim's first Minister of Unification put it, if South Koreans are to improve inter-Korean relations and,

> eventually, create a national community in which such universal values as democracy and the principles of market economy are respected, the North must change. For this reason, we will continue to promote economic cooperation with the North under the principle of separating politics from economic cooperation.[4]

As the depth of North Korean rigidity became more apparent—and perhaps as conservative holdovers like Minister Kang were replaced by others less concerned with "changing" North Korea—this emphasis faded somewhat. But it fed a continuing administration search for signs of "change" in North Korea that would help justify its largess to domestic and foreign critics.

The other core policy component concerns the requirement for reciprocity. In the beginning, the administration took "reciprocity" literally to mean a mutual process of "give and take." Both Koreas would "promote mutual benefits" in inter-Korean relations by respecting each other's opinion and allowing each to gain something from the interactions.[5] Unfortunately, this was another area where

---

[4]"Words from the Minister," *Korean Unification Bulletin*, Vol. 1, No. 1, July 1998 (www.unikorea.go.kr), p. 1. The section "Policy Q & A" that follows these remarks elaborates:

> At the present state, the most realistic policy alternative that can lead to North Korea's gradual transformation is to expand intra-Korean [sic] economic cooperation which North Korea needs most. The promotion of North Korea policy based on this principle will help us to expand economic cooperation between the North and the South and, therefore, contribute in creating an environment that makes North Korea ready to reform itself (ibid., p. 6).

[5]From "Policy Q & A," ibid., p. 5:

theory and practice did not meet. When the administration tried to apply the principle two months after its inauguration by requesting the establishment of a reunion center for families separated since the Korean War in exchange for South Korean fertilizer assistance, the North Koreans denounced their southern counterparts as "horse traders" and cut off all interactions.

Although the administration stuck to its strict quid pro quo position for another year, eventually it dropped this demand and introduced a new notion of "flexible reciprocity." By this it meant not a strict quid pro quo or even a simultaneous process of "give and take." Rather, it meant a "flexible, relative, and time-differential" approach in which the ROK, as the stronger "elder brother," would be patient and allow North Korea to reciprocate South Korean measures at an undetermined time, and in some undetermined way, in the future.[6] "Give first, get something later" is not an inaccurate characterization. Administration leaders further differentiated between humanitarian assistance, which the government would provide without any reciprocal requests at all, and government-to-government economic cooperation in areas like building social infrastructure, for which "flexible reciprocity" would apply. Private-sector trade and strictly commercial assistance, in principle, would be free from any government meddling.

With these basic principles and core policy components set, the administration structured its engagement policy around five sets of activities. The first involves efforts to restart long-suspended talks and expand political dialogue between officials of the two Koreas. This represented the administration's top goal from its inception.

Initially, administration leaders focused on trying to reactivate the Basic Agreement of 1991. Toward this end, they sought an exchange of special envoys to reaffirm both sides' commitment to the landmark agreement and reconfirm their intention to implement its pro-

---

In the intra-Korean [sic] relations, too often engulfed by mutual mistrust, the most efficient way to prevent unnecessary rivalry and to promote mutual benefits for both Koreas would be a more pragmatic, give-and-take approach. This is why we need to stress the principle of reciprocity.... In principle, the principle of reciprocity applies to every aspect of North Korea policy of our government.

[6]Yang Young-shik, op. cit., pp. 54–55.

visions. But the administration made clear that a summit meeting between the top leaders of the two Koreas was its ultimate objective. When North Korea made equally clear that it was opposed to including reactivation of the Basic Agreement as part of any summit's agenda, the administration dropped this goal completely. In turn, North Korea dropped its opposition to a summit, which led to President Kim's historic visit to North Korea in June 2000.[7] The summit meeting stimulated in turn a series of inter-Korean ministerial talks and other political exchanges. It also generated talk of reaching broader political inter-Korean agreements—perhaps including a formal peace declaration—in the context of a return visit by North Korean leader Kim Jong Il to Seoul.

The administration has been careful to emphasize that such efforts to expand political dialogue cannot come at the expense of deterrence. Rather, in line with the sunshine policy's first basic principle, it has repeatedly stressed that South Korea will *simultaneously* maintain a strong deterrent posture toward the North and pursue efforts to reduce tension through political dialogue. In practice, however, the administration has often appeared to give priority to the latter when the two simultaneous goals have come into conflict. It has shown particular reluctance to take military risks (e.g., responding to low-level North Korean military provocations) or other steps (e.g., holding traditional celebrations to commemorate the anniversary of the Korean War) that might upset North Korea and provoke Pyongyang to suspend political dialogue.

The sunshine policy's second set of activities is geared toward expanding North-South economic intercourse. This involves a range of efforts within South Korea itself, such as encouraging South Korean businessmen to visit the North, lifting the ceiling on the magnitude

---

[7]The agreed-upon agenda for the summit meeting, negotiated between representatives of the two governments in five preparatory meetings between April 8 and May 18, 2000, makes no mention of the Basic Agreement. Instead, it simply states that the agenda will be

> to reconfirm the three basic principles for unification of the country enunciated in the historic July 4 [1972] South-North Joint Communiqué, and discuss the issues of the reconciliation and unity, exchanges and cooperation, and peace and unification of the people.

The agreement may be found in the ROK government white paper entitled *Peace and Cooperation*, April 2001, and is available online at www.unikorea.go.kr.

of investment allowed in the North, and simplifying ROK legal procedures to facilitate expanded South Korean economic undertakings. It also involves a search for agreements with the North on such things as preventing double taxation and guaranteeing investments that are essential for enhancing economic interactions.

Ostensibly, expanded economic cooperation is intended to benefit both Koreas. But the administration has been explicit that it will focus first on areas most important to the North, partly because of Seoul's superior economic position and partly because of Pyongyang's paranoia about South Korean "penetration." One example is the Hyundai group's tourism and development project at Mt. Kumgang in the North, which the administration has heralded as a major success of its sunshine policy despite the project's financial nonviability. Another is the large-scale joint venture to develop an industrial complex in the Kaesong area of North Korea. A third is the agreement to reconnect the railway between Seoul and Shinuijoo. The administration sees such projects as addressing Pyongyang's crushing economic needs, while facilitating further economic interactions and contributing to reduced tensions on the peninsula. It also sees such projects as building blocks toward the creation of a "South-North economic community," a single joint economic sphere that would help propel the development over time of a broader sociocultural community.

The third set of activities focuses on fostering reunions and exchanges between families separated by the Korean War. This has been one of the sunshine policy's top priorities. As noted above, the administration sought unsuccessfully early in its term to use this issue as a test case for its core policy of "reciprocity," proposing to swap fertilizer for the establishment of a reunion center for separated families. It has pressed hard since then for North Korean concessions on other humanitarian exchanges, fueling a series of interministerial and Red Cross Society talks to organize family exchange visits. And it has formally defined "separated families" broadly to include not only civilians and prisoners of war but also others abducted to the North since the Korean War who remain in North Korea. North Korea's agreement in the summit's joint declaration to "promptly resolve humanitarian issues such as exchange visits by separated family members and relatives," and the three exchanges of

100 families each, can accurately be seen as a result of South Korean pressure.

Providing food and other humanitarian assistance is the sunshine policy's fourth set of activities. Food aid represents both a potential source of South Korean leverage over North Korea, given the latter's desperate agricultural and nutritional situation, and required "buy-in" to keep Pyongyang at the table. Recognizing this dual nature, the administration has from the beginning emphasized its willingness to be generous in providing North Korea significant amounts of emergency relief and other food assistance, through both international organizations and direct government-to-government channels. It has provided Pyongyang fertilizer, seeds, and pesticides, for example, to improve North Korean agricultural production. It has contributed pharmaceuticals to fight potential epidemics and other infectious diseases resulting from North Korea's severe nutritional and health care deficiencies. And it has actively encouraged South Korea's private sector and other civilian organizations to provide additional food, fertilizer, and humanitarian assistance. The administration has clearly recognized the need for more fundamental, systemic changes in North Korea if its chronic food shortage is to be resolved. North Korean rigidity and resistance, however, have hindered major South Korean policy initiatives in this area.

The sunshine policy's fifth set of activities involves broader efforts to encourage international cooperation to reduce tensions and maintain peace on the peninsula. The administration has adhered to its commitment under the U.S.-DPRK Agreed Framework to provide North Korea with light-water nuclear reactors—despite the crushing financial crisis and subsequent economic slowdown in the ROK— and to playing a central role in KEDO, the international consortium that provides energy assistance to North Korea. It has tried to use the "Four Party Talks" to draw North Korea into discussions about military confidence building measures and ways to transition from the current military armistice to a permanent peace agreement. It has also sought to initiate some kind of multilateral regional security forum that would include North Korea and focus on means for reducing tensions on the Korean Peninsula. Most strikingly, the administration has actively encouraged its friends and allies to expand ties with North Korea, while enthusiastically promoting North Korean participation in both regional and international organizations.

To be sure, these five sets of activities draw from, and/or build on, important aspects of previously existing policy. The emphases on peaceful coexistence, promoting economic cooperation and humanitarian exchange, the simultaneous need for political dialogue and continued deterrence, and the importance of a gradual, "independent" process of reconciliation are all products of a long evolutionary process. So too is the stress on summitry and sustained high-level government-to-government discussions. President Kim's formal adherence to the unification formula worked out by his predecessors represents at least tacit recognition of the basic underlying continuity in South Korean policies.

It is possible that greater public acknowledgment of these continuities might have helped generate broader public support for the new administration's policies. This has not been the administration's general tendency, however. On the contrary, it has worked hard to differentiate its policies from those of its predecessors, largely ignoring their shared roots and objectives. President Kim personally passed up a major opportunity to build a wider base of political support at the time he was awarded the Nobel Peace Prize. While he used his acceptance speech to thank all those who have supported him over the years—and separately expressed the wish to share his prize with the North Korean leader—he failed to even note the efforts of his South Korean predecessors to bring about peaceful coexistence. The administration's extreme personalization of policy and marked tendency to accentuate the differences between it and previous governments have been conspicuous features of its public diplomacy.

Even had this tendency been less pronounced, however, it would not have altered the real and numerous differences between President Kim's approach to engagement and that of his predecessors. These include, in particular, the substitution of "reconciliation" for "unification" as the sunshine policy's operative objective, the insistence on separating economics from politics, the de facto jettisoning of reciprocity as a central policy component, and the priority given to helping North Korea. Other important differences concern the way in which policy has been implemented. These differences include the consistency, eagerness, and speed with which the administration has sought to engage North Korea; the emphasis it has given to sustaining political dialogue, even at risk to other important ROK security objectives; the trust it has been willing to place in North Korea's leaders, often without clear evidence of the basis for this trust; and the willingness it has demonstrated to act unilaterally without first securing domestic support. Together, these differences represent significant departures from traditional South Korean policy.

Underlying the administration's novel approach are several critical assumptions. These form something of a logic chain motivating government policy. In essence, the administration has predicated its policies on the calculation of the following:

- *North Korea's rhetoric and bellicosity mask what is fundamentally a survival strategy.*

- *Providing assurances of its survival—politically, economically, and militarily—will produce significant changes in North Korea.*

- *A serious, sustained process of providing North Korea such assurances and inducing such changes will increase North Korean dependence on South Korea and on the outside world more broadly.*

- *Increased North Korean dependence will both temper Pyongyang's behavior and maximize South Korean control over all issues dealing with North Korea.*

- *Even in the absence of this kind of process, North Korea will not collapse.*

- *Engaging the North and convincing it of South Korea's sincere intentions is the only viable alternative to high tensions and conflict on the peninsula.*

The debate in South Korea today is a product of sharp differences over both the new policy departures and their underlying assumptions. What makes the debate so volatile, however, is the way in which it subsumes, and intensifies, long-standing, unresolved societal tensions and divisions. The next chapter examines both of these features.

Chapter Four

THE PUBLIC DEBATE: ISSUES AND UNDERLYING DIVISIONS

By its nature, public debate is a mixture of elements: the passionate and the partisan, the piddling and the profound. South Korea's debate over the government's dealings with North Korea is no exception, containing elements ranging from the constructive and sincere to the purely self-serving. But at its base are some big questions: Should South Korea seek to engage the North at all? If so, what should be the aim of these efforts? How should this aim be balanced against other important national objectives? What is the efficacy of inducements for a system like North Korea's? How should the murky situation in the North and the regime's erratic behavior be interpreted, and what criteria should be used to evaluate the effectiveness of alternative South Korean approaches? The answers to these questions, by their nature, are not self-evident.

A point of departure might be to think of the South Korean debate as a layer cake—a single, solid object on the outside but one composed of multiple, overlapping layers on the inside. The center, or heart, of the debate corresponds to the cake's middle ("central") layer. This consists of issues pertaining to the nature of the sunshine policy itself. Although these issues are sometimes obscured by particular topical concerns, they constitute much of the essence, and influence much of the texture, of public discussion. Above this layer is a top layer of specific issues that shift from time to time in response to developments. Many of these issues have dealt with the June 2000 North-South summit and its residue, although some deal with other important topical matters. At the bottom or base layer is a third set of issues emerging from long-standing, unresolved societal tensions and national divisions. These provide certain constants to the public debate and represent fundamental fault lines in the South Korean body politic.

Because of its importance for understanding the public debate, the central, "middle" layer of issues pertaining to the nature of the sunshine policy will be examined first. This will be followed by a look at some more specific, topical issues closer to the surface. The examination will then turn to the debate's most underlying components at the base.

CENTRAL ISSUES

The issues at the center of the debate span almost all aspects of the sunshine policy—its substantive components, operational characteristics, and motivating assumptions. These three aspects provide a framework for viewing the debate's central issues.

Substantive Components

Substantively, South Koreans are divided over everything from the goals of the sunshine policy to the policy's costs and perceived effectiveness. In particular, however, the debate revolves heavily around four key issues.

The first concerns a basic question: What should any move toward greater association with North Korea be all about? As noted in Chapter Three, the administration substituted "reconciliation" for "unification" as the operative goal of its new sunshine policy, although it presented this policy as one that would bring unification closer. It also moved away from South Korea's traditional emphasis on universal values like freedom, democracy, and human rights as the *raison d'être* of its unification efforts toward more nationalistic, "one nation" kinds of notions. These departures generated controversy from the beginning of the administration. Their initial impact was mitigated, however, by South Korea's severe financial crisis and the administration's own decision to maintain the official unification formula developed by President Kim's predecessors. The financial crisis diminished public interest in rapid reunification, which the administration's emphasis on "reconciliation and cooperation" rather than "unification" appealed to. Maintenance of his predecessors' official unification schema palliated long-standing doubts in opposition quarters about President Kim's personal political proclivities.[1] But the North-South summit, and its final Joint Declaration in particular, brought the impact of these departures fully to the surface.

The particular point of contention is the Joint Declaration's statement (Item 2) that there are "common elements" in the unification formulae of the two Koreas and its indication that both sides officially agreed to pursue national unification on the basis of these common elements.[2] The administration and its supporters see this part of the Joint Declaration as one of the major results of the summit. By acknowledging that there are "common elements" in their respective approaches, they believe, the two Koreas have considerably narrowed the gap between them on how to proceed with inter-Korean relations. More importantly, by agreeing to pursue unification on the basis of these "common elements," North Korea has effectively ratified its agreement to postpone unification in favor of peaceful coexistence.

The problem is that this item contains an allusion to a central component of North Korea's historic approach—the formation of a North-South "federation"—that South Koreans have always understood as being aimed at undermining their system and bringing about unification on North Korean terms. Agreeing on this terminology raised questions about whether South Korea had moved away from its own long-standing policy and effectively bought into the North Korean line. It also called into question the administration's intended direction—particularly its commitment to South Korea's traditional insistence on liberal democracy as the essential ideologi-

---

[1]Over the decades as a leader of South Korea's "progressive," opposition forces, President Kim had generated much personal animosity within conservative, establishment circles and open concern over his allegedly "leftist" leanings. Indeed, as described in Chapter Two, these alleged leanings repeatedly landed Kim in prison—and almost cost him his life. In terms of dealings with North Korea, they fostered widespread suspicion within the traditional South Korean elite about Kim's "socialist" orientation and his willingness to forsake liberal democratic values on behalf of unity with North Korea. This is discussed further later in this chapter.

[2]For an English language text of the Joint Declaration, see "Major Agreements in Inter-Korean Relations—Inter-Korean Summit" at www.unikorea.go.kr.

cal foundation for any unified Korean nation. In the process, it revived questions about what the appropriate basis should be for the government's efforts to achieve greater degrees of association with North Korea.[3] The administration's sudden switch from talking only about "peaceful coexistence" to raising the issue of "unification" reinforced these questions.

Such questions may seem somewhat theological, given the seemingly small prospect of peaceful unification by negotiation anytime soon. But even the Kim Dae Jung government has portrayed engagement as only an interim step on the road to eventual unification. In a land divided for over 50 years into two competing ideological systems, and in a land where the Communist North has maintained an unwavering commitment to subverting the democratic, free-market South and bringing the entire peninsula under its control, where this road is leading matters. Such ideological and philosophical questions, moreover, go to the heart of public attitudes about the role and purpose of state governance.[4] As such, they are very sensitive issues.

Not surprisingly, this provision of the Joint Declaration resuscitated latent suspicions about President Kim's personal political orientation. It also fanned smoldering criticism of both the low priority given to North Korea's abysmal human rights situation—despite the president's reputation as a champion of democracy and human rights—and the administration's reluctance to include the issues of North Korean refugees or past terrorist activities on its negotiating agenda.[5] In the process, the provision generated intense debate over

---

[3]For a more elaborate account, see Chung-in Moon, "The Sunshine Policy and the Korean Summit: Assessments and Prospects," *East Asian Review*, Vol. 12, No. 4, Winter 2000, pp. 24–26. Moon, who traveled to Pyongyang as a member of the South Korean summit delegation, indicates that Kim Jong Il "took the initiative" on this issue, "urging President Kim to adopt the North Korean proposal of the *Koryo* Confederal Democratic Republic (namely federation model) as a gift to the entire Korean nation." He sees the "convergence" between the two leaders at the summit on this issue as "one of the most significant achievements in the summit talk," although he suggests this very "sensitive" issue was the "most hotly debated."

[4]Chung-Wook Chung, "Has North Korea Really Changed?" *Korea Focus*, Vol. 9, No. 2, March–April 2001.

[5]See, for example, Min Bok Lee, "Human Rights in North Korea," *Korea Focus*, Vol. 9, No. 3, May–June 2001; and Hyun-ho Kim, "North Korean Refugees Also Deserve 'Sunshine,'" *Korea Focus*, Vol. 9, No. 4, July–August 2001.

the nature and direction of government policy. The administration's failure to describe how the unification approaches of the two Koreas are *different*, or at least explain what is *common* about the two Koreas' images of a unified state, further heightened the debate's intensity.

The second key issue concerns the importance and role of reciprocity in dealing with North Korea. Some South Koreans question the administration's decision to drop reciprocity as a requirement for improving North-South relations on the grounds of principle. To them, all relationships between equal parties should as a matter of course involve reciprocal gains and concessions, and not insisting on such reciprocal exchanges is both morally wrong and politically demeaning. Others focus on the propriety of the decision in the context of North Korea's continuing threatening behavior. To those of this view, it is simply inappropriate to continue extending conciliatory gestures amidst repeated North Korean military provocations—as the administration allegedly has done in the face of North Korean submarine intrusions, insertions of armed commandos, and continuing efforts to develop weapons of mass destruction.

The principal focus of debate on this issue, however, is on the *practical* effects of the administration's decision. Here, critics of the sunshine policy make a range of arguments.[6] They argue, for example, the following:

- "One-sided" concessions do not persuade the North of South Korea's "sincerity" but only encourage Pyongyang to seek additional South Korean concessions.

- A policy based solely on "carrots" and no "sticks" weakens public support for continued engagement with the North, while it provides Pyongyang both incentives and opportunities to disrupt South Korean politics and undermine the country's political stability.

- The absence of some kind of linkage between South Korean assistance to the North and North Korean willingness to address

---

[6]For a summary, see Rinn-Sup Shinn, "South Korea: 'Sunshine Policy' and Its Political Context," *CRS Report for Congress*, RL30188, February 12, 2001, pp. 17–18.

priority issues on South Korea's agenda decreases the government's credibility with North Korean leaders, as well as its leverage over their actions.

- An appearance of treating security issues lightly by not responding forcefully to North Korean provocations risks generating new problems in South Korea's relationships with the United States and Japan and exacerbating the task of managing allied relations.

What the absence of reciprocity will not do, these critics argue, is induce North Korea to change either its system or behavior. It can therefore advance neither of the government's two principal objectives: resolving the Korean conflict and paving the way to peaceful unification.[7]

The administration has responded to such arguments by emphasizing the importance of "consistency" in dealing with North Korea, contrasting its performance with the alleged irresolution and policy flip-flops of the preceding Kim Young Sam administration. It has also urged South Koreans to be patient, to maintain a long-term perspective, and—befitting the stronger, elder brother—to focus on the "forest" of significant progress in North-South relations rather than the "trees" of periodic North Korean provocations and other bad behavior.[8] Administration leaders point to the summit, Mt. Kumgang project, separated family exchanges, and growing range of inter-Korean contacts and agreements as evidence that its policy is "working."

To critics, on the other hand, the administration's retreat on reciprocity suggests weakness, not strength, and encourages precisely the kinds of behavior the sunshine policy was meant to terminate. Reinforced by the sunshine policy's insistence on a separation of economics and politics, they believe the absence of reciprocity simply communicates an unwillingness to hold the North accountable for its bad behavior. "Naïve appeasement," "appeasement only," and

---

[7]Chung-in Moon, "Understanding the DJ Doctrine: The Sunshine Policy and the Korean Peninsula," in Chung-in Moon and David Steinberg, eds., *Kim Dae-Jung Government and Sunshine Policy* (Yonsei University Press, 1999), p. 51.

[8]Rinn-Sup Shinn, op. cit., p. 18.

"one-sided appeasement" are variations of formulations they often use to characterize the essence of administration policy.[9]

The third key issue in the debate has to do with the sunshine policy's priority on helping North Korea. One aspect of this issue concerns the scale of South Korean assistance. By most measures, the totality of South Korean economic engagement with North Korea would not appear particularly burdensome. According to government figures, for example, South Korea provided Pyongyang less than $230 million in combined government and private assistance in the first three years of the Kim Dae Jung administration (March 1998–April 2001), compared to $284 million in the preceding period (June 1995–February 1998).[10] Also, the amount invested in the North is a minuscule portion of what South Korea has invested in its own economy. In absolute terms, however, South Korea's economic stakes are large and growing, and North Korea's needs are seemingly endless. With South Korea's economic slowdown, continuing financial turmoil, and numerous unmet socioeconomic needs, critics see the government's emphasis on helping the North as representing a serious case of misplaced priorities. Some believe the administration is sacrificing the nation's welfare for its own personal political interests.

Another aspect concerns not the scale but nature of South Korean economic engagement. The lightening rod here is the Hyundai Group's Mt. Kumgang tourism project, which the administration has repeatedly held up as a signal success of its sunshine policy. This project involves a commitment by Hyundai to provide the North over $12 million a month—an amount totaling nearly $1 billion for the more than six years covered by the agreement—in exchange for the

---

[9]Even the most moderate of South Korea's three major conservative newspapers, the *JoongAng Ilbo,* has expressed this view. See, for example, its editorial "A Time to Reexamine the Administration's North Korea Policy" in the August 21, 2001 edition.

[10]The Ministry of Unification, *Toward an Era of Peace and Cooperation* (The Korean Information Service, June 2001), p. 50.

rights to develop a North Korean tourist facility.[11] Already, well over $150 million has been transferred to North Korea, a significant sum for a country as destitute as North Korea.

Critics find major faults with this kind of assistance beyond the magnitude of its financial transfers. For one thing, the project involves cash payments, and the project agreement provides neither any restrictions nor control mechanisms over their use by North Korea. Such payments can thus be allocated however the North Korean regime wants, including for the acquisition of tanks, missiles, long-range artillery, and weapons of mass destruction. In addition, the Mt. Kumgang project involves activities far removed from North Korean population centers. This significantly limits opportunities for human discovery—a critical requirement for encouraging long-term change in North Korea—as South Korean investors, workers, and tourists are kept isolated from their northern counterparts. Finally, critics argue, the project sets a bad precedent. With its large payments and loose terms, the project raises expectations in Pyongyang unrealistically high while lowering the bargaining power of other potential South Korean investors.

The fourth key issue concerns the actual benefits South Korea derives from the sunshine policy. To some extent, this issue derives logically from the other substantive issues. A policy that is geared toward communicating sincerity and fostering reconciliation, that focuses on helping North Korea and bolstering the regime's confidence that it can survive, and that forecloses linkages or conditions that might impede the flow of bilateral interactions will almost inevitably raise questions about payback. The issue is simple: What's in it for us? Almost any debate over costs, moreover, invariably raises questions about benefits.

But in another sense this issue stands alone. At its most basic, the issue concerns the question of effectiveness—the extent to which the

---

[11]The monthly payments have been scaled back unilaterally by Hyundai because of its severe liquidity crunch, and the basis for calculating the payments to the North has been modified. Meanwhile, the South Korean government has stepped in and become, in effect, a full partner in trying to rescue the project, which it considers extremely high in political importance—if low in economic feasibility. Youngdae Song, "Ill-Advised Assistance for Mt. Kumgang Tourism Project," *Korea Focus*, Vol. 9, No. 4, July–August 2001.

government's policy furthers important ROK interests. Clearly there has been very little economic payback thus far from South Korea's engagement: Not a single South Korean firm has made any money in North Korea and few expect this to happen any time soon.[12] The debate has focused, therefore, on two other measures of effectiveness. Both relate to objectives long high on South Korea's policy agenda.

The most important is the effectiveness of the sunshine policy in reducing the North Korean threat and improving South Korean security. As reflected in the sunshine policy's very first principle, the administration has given strong verbal emphasis to maintaining a credible, effective deterrent, and it has stressed the government's intention to maintain both the U.S.-ROK alliance and U.S. military presence toward this end. Officials have also credited administration policy with having generated increased trust between the two Koreas, thereby reducing tensions on the peninsula. A new willingness on the part of North Korea to accept the U.S. military presence in South Korea, they emphasize, is a further product of the government's policy.[13]

Critics of the sunshine policy, however, see it otherwise. To many of them, the balance between "reconciliation" and "security" has been overwhelmingly on the side of the former. While the administration

---

[12]As of October 2000, 96 percent ($4.1 billion) of the total South Korean investment planned in the North ($4.3 billion) was accounted for by the light water reactor project provided under the terms of the U.S.-DPRK Agreed Framework. Hyundai's Mt. Kumgang project accounted for roughly 87 percent of the remaining $171 million. As a result of North Korea's failure to abide by the agreements it signed with other South Korean companies for the rest (roughly $26 million), these companies have been unable to continue their operations in the North or even recoup the $6.2 million they already invested. Hyundai's own financial difficulties make completing even the Mt. Kumgang project uncertain—let alone finding the funds to begin other large intended projects like the industrial complex at Kaesong. See Young-Yoon Kim, "Investment for Balanced Growth Between North and South Korea," *Korea Focus*, Vol. 9, No. 1, January–February 2001.

[13]The administration has claimed that Kim Jong Il agreed with President Kim during their private summit talks that the United States should maintain its military presence in Korea. The North Koreans themselves are telling a somewhat different story. After listening to President Kim describe the domestic difficulties this issue causes him in South Korea, they insist, Kim Jong Il simply indicated his understanding of the difficulties President Kim described and his willingness to put off discussion of this issue for now.

has said many of the right words, they contend, in practice it has given priority to engagement over security, as reflected in its repeated efforts to save North Korea's face and overlook North Korean military provocations. Indeed, it is hard to say if critics are more indignant at these repeated North Korean provocations or at the administration's tendency to turn the other cheek. Arguing that such responses undermine South Korea's psychological preparedness, erode deterrence, and encourage yet more North Korean provocations, they harshly criticize the administration for its alleged "neglect" of national security. Some characterize this neglect as "gross irresponsibility."[14]

At the same time, they argue, security issues have ranked far too low on the administration's negotiating agenda. The Joint Declaration issued after the North-South summit, for example, failed to even mention the word "security" and avoided addressing any critical military issue at all, as did the sole meeting between North and South Korean Defense ministers in September 2000. At a minimum, critics charge, administration leaders acted inappropriately in acceding to North Korean wishes to keep security issues off the summit and Defense minister meeting agendas. At a maximum, they allowed the focus on reconciliation—and particularly on a "common" theoretical approach to unification—to completely overwhelm the need to establish a practical system for reducing military tensions and building peace on the peninsula.

Meanwhile, many critics point out, North Korea's military buildup continues, as does the priority it gives to building a "militarily powerful" state. Not only did the summit fail to generate a slowdown in North Korean military activities—the procurement of arms has actually increased, while the percentage of forward-deployed forces has continued to grow—but North Korea followed up the summit by conducting its most extensive military exercises in a decade.[15] Many South Koreans echo the view of U.S. General Thomas Schwartz, commander of U.S.-ROK Combined Forces in Korea, who noted in

---

[14]Jin-hyun Paik, "Violation of South Korea's Territorial Waters," *Korea Focus*, Vol. 9, No. 3, May–June 2001.

[15]Taewoo Kim, "Sunshine Policy and ROK-U.S. Alliance," *The Korean Journal of International Studies*, Vol. XXVIII, No. 1, Fall/Winter 2001, p. 140.

congressional testimony that North Korean military forces over the past year have grown "bigger, better, closer, and deadlier."[16] Neither do critics of the sunshine policy believe the administration's assertion that North Korea now accepts the U.S. military presence. They cite as supporting evidence not merely continuing North Korean propaganda denouncing the U.S. presence but the joint communiqué issued after Kim Jong Il's August 2000 visit to Moscow—which once again explicitly called for the withdrawal of all U.S. military forces from Korea.

More broadly, critics argue that Pyongyang's insistence on dealing only with the United States on security issues proves that its central strategic objectives remain intact. What Pyongyang wants is to sign a bilateral peace agreement with the United States that will lead to the withdrawal of U.S. forces and the ultimate reunification of Korea on North Korean terms. North Korea's decision to suspend the inter-Korean dialogue altogether for over seven months in 2001 and focus on developing relations with Russia and China—which many South Koreans saw as an effort to gain leverage for future talks with the United States—reinforced this interpretation. Such actions demonstrate, they argue, that the sunshine policy has failed to either alter North Korea's calculus or improve South Korea's security. Together with North Korea's demonstrated willingness to pull the rug out from under President Kim, as Kim Jong Il did in his visit to Moscow, these actions also undermine the argument that the sunshine policy has produced a basis for greater "trust" between the two Koreas.

The other measure of effectiveness concerns South Korea's long-standing goal of inducing Pyongyang to end its attempts at subversion and accept the ROK government as an equal partner. On its face, Kim Jong Il's agreement to meet with President Kim for summit talks and, in principle, visit Seoul for a follow-up summit suggests a historic breakthrough in achieving this goal, as does his respectful treatment of the official South Korean delegation in Pyongyang. The range of official inter-ministerial talks in which North Korea has participated and the increasingly lengthy list of interactions to which it has formally committed itself further bolster this impression.

---

[16]*Statement of General Thomas A. Schwartz, Commander in Chief United Nations Command/Combined Forces Command & Commander, United States Forces in Korea Before the Senate Armed Services Committee, March 27, 2001.*

At the same time, however, North Korea has failed to honor almost all of these commitments. Despite his public pledge, for example, Kim Jong Il has failed to follow through on his promise to visit Seoul—more than two years since the June 2000 summit—despite increasingly plaintive pleading by South Korean leaders.[17] Indeed, between June 2000 and June 2002 North Korea kept only one of the more than 20 commitments it made in official government-to-government meetings to improve North-South relations—and that (concerning meetings of separated families) it kept only partly.[18] Pyongyang's continuing erratic behavior has called into question its willingness to come to terms with South Korea more broadly. The regime has toyed with the ROK government, for example, by repeatedly canceling scheduled meetings—often at the last minute and without any explanation—and by belatedly insisting on artificial conditions for agreed-upon interactions that humiliate administration leaders and undercut their positions with the South Korean public. Also, most damaging, North Korea has made no pretense of having discarded its traditional "united front" strategy, which seeks to enlist South Korean dissidents, "progressives," and other citizens in supporting North Korean policy positions in an effort to undermine the ROK government.[19] Inviting South Korean nongovernment groups to North Korea for politically charged activities, while simultaneously refusing to deal with ROK government officials, further strengthened the critics' argument that, in reality, Pyongyang

---

[17]In one month alone this year, President Kim publicly urged Kim Jong Il to visit Seoul eight times. Jin Woo Chun, "Overemphasis on Kim Jong Il's Visit to Seoul," *Dong-A Ilbo*, June 18, 2001.

[18]Brent Choi, "Kim Jong-il: Promises, Promises," an English translation of an article published originally in the *JoongAng Ilbo*, June 1, 2001.

[19]Pyongyang successfully enticed South Korean labor unions, for example, to draft a joint manifesto calling for a unification formula that endorses the North's traditional position. It then labeled South Koreans who supported the manifesto "advocates of unification" and denounced South Korean critics as being "anti-unification." Such activities violate North Korea's explicit pledge in the summit's Joint Declaration to employ talks between the official authorities of the two governments as the vehicle for North-South dialogue. Not surprisingly, they also are seen by many South Koreans as blatant attempts to drive a wedge between the ROK government and its citizens and destabilize South Korean society. See "Pyongyang's Manipulations," an editorial in the English edition of the *JoongAng Ilbo*, July 26, 2001.

accepts neither the Republic of Korea nor the goal of peaceful coexistence on the peninsula.[20]

Having said this, even critics of the president's policy acknowledge certain successes. The summit is nearly universally seen as a historic breakthrough, and the four family reunions that took place at least begin to address an equally universal yearning for renewed family contact after five decades of separation. Most South Koreans credit the president for these achievements, as well as for the consistency he has maintained in implementing his policy. Having said that, few of these accomplishments are the measures of effectiveness most critics adopt to evaluate his performance.[21]

Operational Characteristics

These substantive aspects of the sunshine policy are the focal points of debate but—reflecting South Korea's significant progress in democratization perhaps—there is also substantial criticism of the way in which policy has been fashioned and implemented. The major point of contention has to do with the openness and transparency of the policymaking process. To be sure, secretive, centralized decisionmaking is hardly unique to the current Korean government. Korea's political tradition and culture have frequently given government policy a top-down, authoritarian quality. Also, given the objective threat North Korea has posed to South Korean security, han-

---

[20]North Korea's crass political manipulation of the August 15, 2001, commemoration of Korea's "liberation" from Japanese colonial rule was particularly egregious. While refusing to participate in any joint activity with, or sending its own delegation to, South Korea, Pyongyang invited a large number of South Korean nongovernmental groups to North Korea where—violating another explicit pledge—it induced many to participate in an activity demonstrating support for the North Korean regime. The impact in South Korea was huge and immediate: Delegation members were arrested upon their return to Seoul, the architect of South Korea's sunshine policy was forced to resign, and President Kim's coalition government was toppled. For details, see Donald G. Gross, "President Kim and His Sunshine Policy: Twisting in the Wind" and Aidan Foster-Carter, "Back on Track?" both of which are in *Comparative Connections* October 2001, an electronic journal put out by Pacific Forum CSIS (www.csis.org/pacfor/ccejournal.html).

[21]One respected journalist, for example, derided the president early on for giving the impression that he is "more concerned about the consistency and rationale of his policy than about its effectiveness." See Dae-joong Kim, "The Difference Between 'Sunshine' and 'Sunshine Only,'" *Korea Focus*, Vol. 7, No. 4, July–August 1999.

dling inter-Korean relations has always required a certain degree of secrecy and governmental prerogative. Most South Koreans are willing to give the administration significant latitude in formulating policy.

Still, many argue that policymaking in the Kim Dae Jung administration has been excessively closed and opaque. They criticize the administration, for example, for allowing policies toward the North to be made by a handful of individuals largely shielded from public view, failing to inform the public about either the content of government deliberations or the bases for measures adopted by government bodies, and making unilateral decisions without required legislative approval or oversight.[22] President Kim's summit agreement with Kim Jong Il on "common elements" for a shared unification formula without prior parliamentary endorsement or even rudimentary public discussion provoked particularly strong reactions. Notwithstanding its rhetorical stress on the importance of a "national consensus," critics charge, the administration has been noninclusive, intolerant of divergent views, and unresponsive to public opinion. It also launched a major attack on the nation's major newspapers—which was widely understood to be motivated in part by a desire to stifle views critical of the sunshine policy—while it funded and used like-minded civil groups in South Korea to suppress broader political opposition. Such actions reinforce broader questions among the public about the nature and direction of administration policy.

The other major "process" issue has to do with the speed with which the government has sought expanded dealings with North Korea. To many of its critics, the administration has been far too eager for signs of success. For example, it has pushed for steps—such as the establishment of a permanent reunion center in exchange for South Korean fertilizer assistance to the North—that Pyongyang was clearly unprepared to take and that arguably set back or at least delayed efforts to improve bilateral relations. It has also agreed on a wide

---

[22]As one critic put it:

> There have even been instances in which the administration has unilaterally granted and provided food aid to the North without acquiring National Assembly approval for the expenditure of government funds (Chung-Wook Chung, op. cit., p. 6).

range of measures with North Korea on paper, only to find Pyong-yang unwilling to implement them in practice. The administration has demonstrated particular eagerness to have Kim Jong Il honor his commitment to visit Seoul, as noted above, which many critics feel is both unseemly and counterproductive. Given the sharp differences and distrust between the two Koreas, they feel, such haste both decreases South Korean leverage over Pyongyang and increases the risk of damaging other important South Korean interests through ill-considered concessions.

Finally, critics fault the administration for putting all its eggs in one basket. Government leaders have placed such high stakes on rec-onciliation, critics believe, that they have developed no potential response or alternative approach should the basic assumptions underlying the sunshine policy be invalidated. The highly cen-tralized, closed process by which policy is fashioned exacerbates this problem. By insisting on "consistency" behind a single approach and excluding political actors who might have divergent views from participation in the policymaking process, some critics charge, the administration not only limits policy legitimacy but also undermines flexibility in policy choice.[23] This is a mistake in simply tactical terms, they argue, but it can become a much graver strategic error given what they regard as the dubiousness of these motivating assumptions.

Motivating Assumptions

As noted in Chapter Three, President Kim based his administration's approach to North Korea on several basic assumptions and strategic calculations. Debate over the sunshine policy includes most of these assumptions but focuses on the first four in particular.

Assumption number one is that North Korea's harsh rhetoric and ex-treme bellicosity mask what is fundamentally a survival strategy. Many South Koreans simply do not accept this assumption. They

---

[23]Taewoo Kim, op. cit., p. 129:

> For example, if the two Koreas return to confrontation and a change in policy is necessary, policy makers will have difficulty switching to another policy because they lack national consent formed through a pluralistic sys-tem of checks and balance.

understand the seriousness of North Korea's economic situation, of course, and they acknowledge that the regime's top priority is its own survival. But they do not believe that North Korean belligerence derives from a sense of insecurity. Nor do they agree that North Korean leaders use provocative rhetoric and actions as a smoke screen to cover their fear of "absorption." Seeing North Korea's harsh stance and periodic provocations as a defensive response motivated by the regime's "insecurity," they insist, is naïve and misleading.

In fact, these critics argue, North Korea remains fundamentally *offensive* in its orientation. It maintains its unwavering commitment to unification on North Korean terms—as reflected in the regime's continuing insertions of commando forces, periodic probing of the demilitarized zone, and ongoing efforts to undermine the ROK government and destabilize South Korean society. It continues to give overwhelming priority to the military—despite its crushing economic conditions—in order to both achieve its long-term reunification goal and safeguard the short-term security of the North Korean regime. It also refuses to take concrete steps to reduce military tensions on the Korean Peninsula—which would allow a diversion of resources to North Korea's pressing economic needs—or even deal directly with South Korea on security matters lest this legitimate South Korea's role and strengthen its position. None of these policy emphases address North Korea's real needs, critics argue, and all go far beyond what Pyongyang requires to guarantee its survival. South Korean policy, they insist, should be based first and foremost on a "correct" assessment of North Korea's real intentions.

Even if North Korean belligerence did derive from a sense of insecurity, these critics suggest, it is folly to believe that major changes can be produced—as the administration's second assumption posits—by providing "assurances" of the regime's survival. The reason North Korea does not open up and initiate reforms is not because it lacks sufficient "assurances." Rather, it is because the regime understands that any serious move toward opening and reform risks undermining the entire system. Indeed, critics insist, continued isolation and rigid internal controls are not impediments to, but prerequisites for, North Korean survival.

From this perspective, many are perplexed, if not incredulous, at the administration's insistence that North Korea is changing. Not only is

North Korea *not* undergoing significant change, they argue, it *cannot* undergo such change and still survive as a nation. Imagining otherwise is wishful thinking that seriously misunderstands, if not willfully ignores, the very nature of the North Korean system. It is far wiser to predicate policy on a realistic appraisal of this system, they argue, and search for modest movement in those few areas where movement is possible, while giving priority to South Korea's paramount political and security interests.

To those of this persuasion, not surprisingly, the sunshine policy's third and fourth assumptions—that a sustained process of providing assurances will increase North Korea's dependence on South Korea and the outside world, reduce its bellicosity, and temper its behavior—are also problematic. Particularly contentious is the administration's calculation that it can induce Pyongyang to end its hostility and genuinely accept peaceful coexistence with South Korea simply by renouncing "absorption," conveying "sincerity" in desiring reconciliation, and encouraging the United States, Japan, and other countries to normalize relations with North Korea. North Korean leaders will not move decisively in this direction, critics assert, no matter how much "sincerity" is communicated or how much assistance is provided. Indeed, they will simply use such magnanimity to ensure North Korea's survival without making major changes.

To be sure, critics acknowledge the administration's claim that North Korea's military provocations and general hostility have gone down. But they assert that this would have happened with or without the sunshine policy given Pyongyang's need for outside assistance. Whatever the short-term effects of the sunshine policy, therefore, those of this persuasion believe it will not produce fundamental departures in North Korean attitudes and behavior until and unless North Korea gets a different leadership, and/or the pressures become so great as to *compel* systemic changes.

The only basic assumption underlying the sunshine policy that has not been a major part of the South Korean debate is that North Korea is not likely to collapse soon. There are South Koreans, of course, who believe a collapse will eventually happen. Indeed, some believe a collapse is only a matter of time, and/or of increased pressure. As a general statement, however, the debate has not revolved materially around assumptions about North Korea's longevity. Having pre-

dicted the North's collapse for a decade or more, and being preoccupied with South Korea's own internal problems and the potential
costs of any rapid North Korean demise, even many critics of the
sunshine policy are willing to stipulate Pyongyang's continued existence for the foreseeable future.

Accepting this at least short-term possibility, however, is not the
same as accepting the implication drawn by the administration in its
final assumption: Its particular version of engagement is "the only
viable alternative" to high tensions and conflict on the peninsula.
Broadly speaking, three schools of alternative thought may be identified:

- *Benign neglect*: This minority school on the right side of the political spectrum believes that North Korea should be left, essentially, to stew in its own juices. If and when the pressures get
  sufficiently strong, the system will either collapse of its own
  inanity or the regime will be forced to sue for peace on terms
  dictated by South Korea.[24]

- *Tough love*: This much larger group, located somewhere to the
  left of the "benign neglect" school but decidedly to the right of
  the administration, believes that South Korea should engage the
  North but in a very different way than President Kim has. Those
  in this school emphasize that, while there may be certain areas of
  potential cooperation, North Korea is and will remain an enemy.
  They believe, therefore, that tensions are best managed, and the
  danger of conflict best avoided, when South Korea simultaneously emphasizes its own security goals and maintains pressure
  on the North to change its system. Any incentives should be
  linked to concrete North Korean movement in this direction.

- *One people*: This school on the left of the political spectrum generally supports the sunshine policy but believes it has been ham-

---

[24]Those who profess a preference for a more "malign" form of neglect—that is, active
efforts to intensify pressures so as to expedite North Korea's collapse—bolster this
school. Most of those inclined in this more "malign" direction, however, see limited
public support for such efforts, given the potential consequences of a sudden North
Korean collapse. They thus tend to mute their advocacy of this policy preference. Accordingly, they are treated in this book more as general supporters of the "benign neglect" school rather than as representing a separate school of thought—although their
existence should not be ignored.

pered by insufficient attention to North Korea's needs and sensitivities. A lasting reduction of tensions can only happen if South Korea more actively aids Pyongyang, ends its military alliance with the United States and other "threatening" measures, and predicates its unification policies on an "independent" stance reflecting the reality that Koreans are one people.

SPECIFIC ISSUES

In addition to these issues at the center layer, the South Korean debate involves a number of other issues closer to the top relating to more specific concerns or topical developments. The main ones have tended to deal with particular aspects of the June 2000 summit. This is not surprising. The summit was a bombshell in South Korea. Although successive South Korean leaders repeatedly sought a summit meeting over the past 20 years, few South Koreans genuinely expected one to happen anytime soon given Pyongyang's deep antipathy to the ROK and ongoing efforts to "delegitimize" the ROK government. Even less expected was the performance of Kim Jong Il at the summit. Respectful and gracious in public, serious, sophisticated, and well-informed in private, Kim's performance had something of a mind-bending effect in South Korea. Inevitably, this stimulated broad discussion over how to evaluate Kim's performance and assess the implications of his leadership for North Korean policy.

Much of the summit-related debate though has focused on two more specific issues. One concerns the second item of the Joint Declaration stating both sides' agreement to pursue national unification on the basis of the "common elements" in their respective unification approaches. As noted above, this item was highly controversial in South Korea because it was widely seen as reflecting the North's agenda, not the South's, and provoked charges that President Kim had been "deceived" into accommodating the North's position.[25] Another more specific aspect of this issue, though, also continues to resonate: *Which* South Korean unification approach does Item 2 allude to when it talks about "common elements" in the two sides' ap-

---

[25]Chung-in Moon, "One Year After the Korean Summit: Constraints, Opportunities, and Prospects," *AEI Update*, June 15, 2001 (American Enterprise Institute, www.aei.org), p. 7.

proaches, and did President Kim act appropriately when he agreed to this statement?[26] This is a complicated issue that requires at least brief elaboration.

As mentioned in Chapter Two, the official ROK unification formula adopted under Roh Tae Woo, and modified only slightly by Kim Young Sam, provides for a gradual, three-stage process. This process includes an interim "commonwealth" stage of "peaceful coexistence" which involves expanded inter-Korean cooperation as sovereign states over an extended period of time. But it does not seek any formal political integration until the final, "unification" stage of this process. In contrast, President Kim's "personal" unification formula includes an interim stage of "confederation" which, while substantively different from the North's concept of federation, implies at least some form of political integration. As also mentioned above, Kim never formally proposed his "personal" approach as the "official" policy of the ROK government. This part of the summit's Joint Declaration thus generated heated debate over the appropriateness of the president's actions in seemingly substituting his personal unification formula for the official government policy—particularly without any prior national discussions or consensus-building efforts.[27]

The other major summit-related issue concerns the fourth item of the Joint Declaration, which records the two sides' agreement to promote "the balanced development of the national economy through economic cooperation." This provision has generated controversy because of two implications. First, if the "balanced" development of the South and North Korean economies is the administration's desired outcome, then really huge amounts of assistance will be required to raise the North Korean economy up to South Korea's level. As noted above, public enthusiasm for such a prospect has declined sharply in South Korea along with the decline in the

---

[26]Dong-bok Lee, "Inter-Korean Summitry," *Korea and World Affairs*, Vol. XXIV, No. 2, Summer 2000, p 220.

[27]This issue joined others cited by opposition forces as examples of the president having "politicized North-South relations" and served for a short while as one of the alleged grounds for considering his impeachment. Hyung-jin Kim, "Opposition Party Says Impeachment of Kim Should be Carefully Considered," *The Korea Herald*, July 26, 2001.

country's rate of growth. Second, promoting development of a "national" economy implies a degree of integration that many Koreans see little basis for or, given the enormous gap between the two economies, have little interest in. Critics of this provision argue that it would be wiser, given the ROK's own economic difficulties, to put priority on the development of the *South Korean* economy.[28] South Korea's continuing economic difficulties has kept this issue smoldering.

The debate also includes a number of other specific issues not directly related to the results of the summit. For example, many South Koreans are harshly critical of the government's agreement to return to Pyongyang North Korean citizens long detained in South Korea without insisting on a return to the ROK of South Korean prisoners of war, fishermen, and kidnapped citizens held in the North. Debate over the absence of any linkage on this issue reinforces broader criticism of the sunshine policy's neglect of reciprocity.

Another example is the administration's push to reconnect railroads linking the South and North. This issue is debated in terms not only of its cost and feasibility but also of its potential security implications. Critics charge that, because such steps require measures like clearing land mines and opening up parts of the demilitarized zone, they should follow rather than precede concrete, negotiated agreements on tension-reduction and confidence-building measures. Seemingly a question of timing and procedure, debate over this issue actually reflects broader substantive differences over the appropriate balance between South Korea's "engagement" and larger security interests.

Similarly, South Korea's June 2000 decision to allow three North Korean cargo ships to transit through its territorial waters set off heated public discussion. The North Korean vessels had entered South Korean territorial waters in the south illegally and then violated the "Northern Limit Line" separating the two Koreas before returning to

---

[28]For a more favorable interpretation of these same points, see Chung-in Moon, "The Sunshine Policy and the Korean Summit: Assessments and Prospects," op. cit., pp. 27–28. Moon also sees in Item 2 a shift in the government view of economic cooperation from being an end in itself to being a *means* for a larger objective: promoting the development of a "national economy."

North Korea—the first instance of such intentional intrusion of both borders since the armistice agreement was signed ending the Korean War. By deciding to allow this passage as a "one-time exception" a day after it happened, the administration opened itself to charges of deviating in a major way from fundamental South Korean security policy without adequately considering the security implications.[29] It also reinforced broader allegations of administration "appeasement" of North Korea.

The nature and salience of such issues fluctuate from time to time. But they invariably share two things in common: They reflect more underlying differences within South Korea; and they intensify debate over the administration's handling of inter-Korean relations.

CORE COMPONENTS

The debate over these two layers of issues, of course, is important in its own right. At a minimum, it impedes consensus on policy toward the North and roils South Korean politics. What makes the debate so volatile and potentially consequential, however, is the way it has opened deeper fissures within the South Korean body politic. These fissures divide South Koreans sharply along political, regional, and ideological lines. They also generate a number of fundamental issues that constitute core components of the debate over dealings with North Korea.

Among the underlying fault lines dividing South Korean society, the ideological divisions are by far the most important. The roots of these divisions can be traced as far back as the 1920s and the after-effects of Japan's brutal suppression of the March 1, 1919, independence demonstrations.[30] In the wake of this suppression, the Korean

---

[29]See, for example, Jin-hyun Paik, "Violation of South Korea's Territorial Waters," *Korea Focus*, Vol. 9, No. 3, May–June 2001.

[30]One of Korea's major misfortunes was the suppression of Korean nationhood in the first two decades of the 20th century, which occurred at precisely the time when nationalist sentiment was first developing among the Korean masses. The March 1 movement demanding independence from Japanese colonial rule was the first manifestation of nationalism on a mass scale and, as such, marked a turning point in modern Korean history. But its suppression generated a sharp ideological divide among Koreans over issues pertaining to national identity and the nature of a future independent state. For a detailed account from which the main points in the paragraph above

independence movement split along ideological lines. One group of moderate nationalist leaders, identifying Korea's lack of sufficient preparation for independence as the principal problem facing the movement, advocated a gradual program of internal development to prepare for future national independence, deferring the fundamental nationalist demand for sovereignty. The other group of younger, more radical nationalists, appalled by the "accommodationist" position of the moderate reformers and heavily influenced by social revolutionary thought following the Russian revolution, sought to mobilize the Korean masses to actively resist Japanese rule and carry out social revolution. Japan's harsh repression, particularly of the radical nationalists, coupled with the universal desire among Koreans for independence from Japanese rule, often obscured this intra-elite conflict. But the ideological schism between the two groups plagued the nationalist movement throughout the ensuing two-and-a-half decades.[31]

Following Japan's defeat in World War II, the sharp differences that had rent the Korean independence movement reappeared in aggravated form, albeit over different issues.[32] Moderate nationalists and "conservatives" sought to set up a democratic republic; radical nationalists, agrarian reformers, Socialists, Communists, and other "progressives" sought to establish a Socialist state. The decision of the outside powers to divide the peninsula; to impose a trusteeship rather than to allow immediate independence; and, as the Cold War settled hard over the Korean Peninsula, to hold separate elections in the South intensified this divide and further polarized Korean elites. Those on the political right supported separate elections and the establishment of a free, capitalist, independent South Korean state backed by U.S. military forces. Those on the left opposed separate elections on the grounds that they would formalize the division of Korea, rejected capitalism because of its perceived inequalities, and sought the reduction or withdrawal of U.S. troops as a means for facilitating peaceful unification. Unlike those on the right, who sought

---

are extracted, see Michael Edson Robinson, *Cultural Nationalism in Colonial Korea, 1920–1925* (University of Washington Press, 1988). For a briefer overview, see John K. Fairbank, Edwin O. Reischauer, and Albert M. Craig, *East Asia: The Modern Transformation* (Houghton Mifflin Company, 1965), pp. 482–483 and pp. 760–765.

[31]Robinson, op. cit., p. 158.

[32]Woo-keun Han, *The History of Korea* (University of Hawaii Press, 1970), p. 498.

an active role for outsiders in strengthening and supporting South Korea, those on the left emphasized nonintervention and the determination of Korea's fate by Koreans themselves. As in the prewar period, strong groups in the political "center" were conspicuous by their absence.[33]

The Korean War and subsequent strong, authoritarian rule by successive South Korean governments did what the formal division of the peninsula and establishment of separate Korean states did not do: They silenced public debate in South Korea. But they did not "resolve" any of the basic issues. As Sung-Joo Han pointed out in his classic analysis of the overthrow of Syngman Rhee, these sharp ideological differences reappeared when political control was relaxed in the early 1960s—contributing to the failure of liberal democracy in that period—and resurface whenever the government loosens its grip.[34] Today represents precisely such a period.

Not surprisingly, the administration's sunshine policy, reinforced by broader political, generational, and attitudinal change in South Korea, has laid bare this underlying fissure. In the process, it is generating intense emotion on many of the issues described above as policy gets refracted through ideological prisms on both sides of the political spectrum. The ideological divide also fuels an "all-or-nothing" orientation—heightening the historic difficulty Koreans have had in reaching compromise—as both sides increasingly see "enemies" where there were once just opponents. Significantly stepped up North Korean efforts to inflame and manipulate South Korean domestic politics reinforce the intensity of the emotions. Critics castigate the administration not only for providing Pyongyang unprecedented entrée into South Korea's internal politics but for its "lukewarm" attitude toward countering the North's crass intervention.[35]

---

[33]Richard C. Allen, op. cit., p. 80.

[34]Sung-Joo Han, *The Failure of Democracy in South Korea* (University of California Press, 1974), p. 5. Also see Han's more recent "The Shifting Korean Ideological Divide," *Policy Forum Online*, July 11, 2000 (Nautilus Institute, www.nautilus.org/fora/security/0005G_Han.html).

[35]Mi-kyoung Kim, "Reconfiguration of the Ideological Divide in South Korea: An Update on the Post-Pyongyang Summit," *Policy Forum Online*, August 1, 2000 (Nautilus Institute, www.nautilus.org/fora/security/0005B_Cha.html).

The intensified ideological discord has also introduced a number of new issues into the debate over the administration's handling of relations with North Korea. These include, for example, whether South Korea should continue to regard the North as a threat, revise its National Security Law and drop all restrictions on nongovernmental interactions with North Korea, and take broader steps to conciliate Pyongyang as a means for assuaging the regime's security anxieties and provoking changes in its hard-line stance toward South Korea. The major issue, however, has to do with the role of the United States and the future of U.S. military forces in Korea.

On this issue, the impetus comes from critics on the left who have long blamed the United States for the bifurcation of the Korean Peninsula—and hence for the resulting Korean War—and for the long perpetuation of national division. These traditional critics, joined by many in a range of new nongovernment organizations (NGOs) pursuing their own organizational interests, see the presence of U.S. forces as unnecessary for South Korea's security and harmful to the sunshine policy's pursuit of inter-Korean reconciliation. Exploiting changed South Korean images of the North in the wake of the North-South summit, they castigate the United States for impeding improvements in relations with North Korea and challenge the long-term need for a U.S.-ROK security alliance. They also demand the withdrawal of U.S. military forces and broader corrections to what they perceive as "inequities" in U.S.-ROK relations.[36] Generally declining threat perceptions increase the public's receptivity to at least some of these criticisms. So too do periodic controversies (e.g., alleged U.S. "atrocities" in the early days of the Korean War, "compensation" for South Koreans killed or injured during the 1980 Kwangju demonstrations demanding an end to martial law, etc.) in South Korea's relations with the United States.

Critics on the other side of the spectrum, on the other hand, denounce the sunshine policy precisely for encouraging such views. They allege that the policy has weakened the public's awareness of the need for national defense, undermining South Korea's defense preparedness and endangering U.S. support for ROK security in the

---

[36]See, for example, Wook-Shik Jung, *Let's Prepare for Korea Without U.S. Forces* (Seoul, 2000); and Won-ung Kim, *SOFA, an Accord of Inequality: Problems and Direction for Revision* (Seoul, 2000).

process. They worry that public threat perceptions will continue to decline and no one in the government will be willing to argue in support of a strong defense. These critics also fault the sunshine policy for stimulating social tensions inside South Korea, including those with a decidedly anti-American tinge. Some see the real danger of a fragmentation of South Korean society, with a "revolutionary-like" atmosphere leading to random acts of violence (e.g., groups vandalizing "pro-American" organizations because they are insufficiently "nationalist" or preventing certain newspapers from being distributed because they are "anti-unification"). Some of them profess to fear that the government might turn a blind eye to such actions.

At this point, such concerns appear exaggerated. It is probably safe to say that the majority of South Koreans, as well as the mainstream in both the ruling and major opposition parties, are opposed to and would constrain random acts of violence. They also understand the importance of the U.S.-ROK relationship and support a continued U.S. military presence and close U.S.-ROK security cooperation. It is probably also safe to say, however, that South Korea is having growing trouble with the ideological extremes on both sides of the political spectrum.

A sharp divide between South Korean regions is a second underlying fissure opened by the sunshine policy. As a major phenomenon affecting national policy, this divide dates to the Park Chung Hee period and President Park's pronounced tilt toward his southeastern home region in both political appointments and resource allocations. As successive governments perpetuated this tilt, South Koreans in Kim Dae Jung's southwestern part of the country—traditionally looked down upon by other Koreans as something of "country bumpkins"—came to feel particularly discriminated against. The process of democratization beginning in the latter 1980s broadened this divide further, as South Korea's political parties each came to take on a particular regional coloration.

Such regional animosities have significantly intensified and deepened since President Kim's inauguration. To some extent, this was probably inevitable. President Kim's election not only involved the transfer of power from the ruling party to the political opposition for the first time in South Korean history, it also involved a shift in attention, and resources, away from South Korea's traditionally dominant region to its most downtrodden. But President Kim has fanned and exacerbated these animosities himself by stocking leadership positions in almost all parts of the South Korean establishment with people from his own region. Some of these people were promoted to top-level positions disregarding traditional bureaucratic practices. Others have little national or governmental experience. And many are former lawyers, scholars, political dissidents, and long-time associates of the president from his days as an opposition leader who tend to have a decidedly more "liberal" orientation toward national policy. Not surprisingly, the competence of these individuals and their ability to protect South Korean security interests as they seek a breakthrough with North Korea have become issues in the debate over the sunshine policy. Also not surprisingly, public opinion polls increasingly show a marked correlation between support for the sunshine policy and regional affiliation, suggesting a growing polarization along regional lines.[37]

Animosity between "pro" and "anti" Kim Dae Jung forces is a third long-standing cleavage in South Korean politics uncovered by the debate over the government's sunshine policy. This is one area where the importance of personality cannot be exaggerated. Put simply, President Kim is a man who generates both intense loyalty and intense antagonism. Part of this, as noted above, is due to the legacy of South Korean rule by military-dominated governments. Along with the reputation Kim acquired during this period as a champion of democracy and human rights, he also acquired a fixed image in much of South Korea's conservative elite as a divisive leader with distinct "socialist" leanings. Another part may be a product of the president's long experience in the difficult world of South Korean opposition politics. As a smart and skilled survivor, he developed an ability to mobilize his allies to pursue his goals without leaving traces

---

[37]A December 26, 2000, poll taken by Gallup, for example, found that an overwhelming 79.4 percent of the people from the southwestern province of Cholla believed that the government's North Korea policy had been well implemented in the six months since the summit, while only 10.7 percent believed it was not well implemented. In contrast, 57.1 percent and 45.8 percent of the people in the southeastern provinces of South and North Kyungsang respectively believed the government's policy had not been well implemented, versus only 34.3 percent and 40.4 percent, respectively, who held the opposite opinion. Asked more broadly about the president's job performance, a majority in all regions other than the Cholla Provinces said he is "not doing a good job."

of his own involvement. Many South Koreans distrust him simply because they cannot predict what he will do next.

But much of these intense feelings stem from actions Kim himself has taken since becoming president. On the North Korea issue, for example, he has pursued policies ("common elements," "federation," "national economy," etc.) that suggest major departures in South Korea's ideological orientation. On domestic issues, he has pursued "reforms" that have actually led to *greater* state intervention in the economy, while he has introduced a range of traditionally "leftist" measures (welfare, teachers unions, etc.) that constitutes entirely new phenomena in South Korean society. In the process, President Kim has heartened supporters but revitalized long-standing suspicions among detractors that he intends to move South Korea toward a socialist system—either as a prelude to, or means for facilitating, unification.

More broadly, even dispassionate observers suggest that President Kim has a tendency to choose rhetoric and actions that, while solidifying support among his allies on the left, effectively validate the suspicions of many conservatives. The president's attack on the South Korean media—allegedly for tax evasion but widely seen as a means to silence critics of his sunshine policy and improve his party's prospects in the following year's presidential election—is one example. His intrusive investigation of Cabinet members and other officials for not only official but also personal wrongdoing—which many opposition figures saw as a precursor of similar investigations of them—is another. A third is his behind-the-scenes support of South Korean NGOs, which few South Koreans believe could have developed so fast without active government encouragement and financial support. These and other steps have stimulated sharp divisions along personal lines. The Nobel Prize award heightened emotions on both sides of this long-standing cleavage, with those personally identified with Kim feeling intense vindication and those who have long hated and distrusted him becoming even more agitated. In this sense, it is not possible to separate the debate over the administration's policy from deeper divisions over its leader.

These underlying fault lines account for much of the visceral quality of the debate over the government's approach to North Korea. They also provide some recurrent themes that run like a leitmotif through historic debates over South Korean policy. By nature, these themes reflect conflicting core values. By subject, they address two fundamental issues:

- *What should be the priority aim of South Korean policy?* Historically, one side of the divide has emphasized the need to focus primarily on strengthening South Korea as an independent state, both to safeguard South Korean interests and to ensure that, when unification comes, it will come on South Korean terms. The other side has stressed the need to overcome national division above all else, even at the risk of diluting South Korean independence.

- *Why should South Korean policy adopt one or the other as its priority objective?* Again, two ideological sides collide over core values. One side has stressed the importance of political and economic freedom, seeing unification as meaningless—or worse—if it means living under North Korea's "Communist," totalitarian system. While unification is important, they believe, it must be the "right kind" of unification. The other side has emphasized the fact that Koreans are racially, culturally, and historically a single people. For many on this side, any type of unification—including unification under a socialist system—is better than continued division. For them, restoring Korea's "people-hood" is the central task of the Korean nation.

Undoubtedly many things help account for the staying power of these underlying fissures. One has to do with Korea's colonial background and long experience under de facto military rule: Put simply, the country has had little time to develop the institutions all democracies need to meld and moderate such sharply conflicting perspectives. Another is the problem of competing nationalisms: Both sides see themselves as the "true" Korean nationalists—one defining nationalism in terms of Korean "people-hood" and class conflict and the other in terms of democracy, free markets, and human rights—and each has long historic roots, and memory, to draw upon. A third is North Korean behavior: Pyongyang's ongoing efforts to manipulate the intra-South Korean competition and destabilize South Korean politics continually inflame the divisions and intensify their impact.[38]

Perhaps the best explanation, though, is the simplest: The fissures remain because the underlying issues have never been resolved. In this sense, the fault lines uncovered by the debate over the government's sunshine policy should not be considered a "legacy" of the past. They are a continuing phenomenon.

---

[38]A good example occurred at the time of long-time Hyundai head Chung Ju-Yung's death. The North Korean delegation that attended his funeral, aware of the South Korean ideological divide, wrote "we're all one people" in the guest book in a blatant attempt to stir up South Korean emotions and reinforce the "left" nationalist tradition.

Chapter Five

INTERNAL DYNAMICS: THE ACTORS

South Koreans often describe their country as a "shrimp among whales," employing an old Chinese saying to describe South Korea's geostrategic position as a small country surrounded by large and powerful neighbors. And there is no question that the major powers—particularly the United States—continue to exert enormous influence on the course of developments on the peninsula, as does North Korea in its own inimitable fashion. Insofar as the debate over policies toward the North is concerned, however, developments *inside* South Korea—the process of democratization and broader social and cultural transition under President Kim Dae Jung in particular—have also been critical. Democratization shattered the formerly monolithic South Korean policy line toward North Korea and opened up the policy process. President Kim's inauguration placed new leaders with very different philosophies and approaches in key positions throughout the South Korean establishment, while shifting the elite's social and ideological center of gravity. In the process, a broader range of political groups, perspectives, and interests came to contend over a more diverse—and in certain instances more fundamental—set of policy issues. This chapter introduces the major actors.

THE GOVERNMENT

The sunshine policy has been defined and directed by two main actors: President Kim and his chief aide, Lim Dong-Won. President Kim, of course, has played the leading role himself. This is a role for which he long prepared as the most "progressive" of the main opposition party leaders. As described in Chapter Two, Kim developed much earlier in his career his own "three-stage approach" to unification, an approach that helped solidify his reputation as a "Communist" among hard-line South Korean conservatives and contributed to his being jailed and sentenced to death in the early 1980s. He sustained his interest in unification throughout his prison years and thereafter, publishing a book on the subject when he was still an opposition leader.[1] In addition, several years before he became president, Kim publicly identified a "sunshine policy" as "the only effective way to deal with isolated countries such as North Korea," albeit in the context of urging the United States to be patient with Pyongyang in resolving the nuclear crisis.[2] In 1995, he described such a policy in detail in another book entitled *Kim Dae Jung's Three Stage Approach to Korean Reunification: Focusing on the South-North Confederal Stage*, although he did not use the term "sunshine policy" to describe his own policy until after his inauguration as president.[3]

Lim Dong-Won is a retired two-star general with considerable experience with unification and foreign policy issues. After his retirement from the military, Lim served as ambassador to Nigeria and Australia during the Chun administration. Between 1988 and 1992, he participated directly in Roh Tae Woo's reconciliation and cooperation policy toward North Korea in a variety of positions.[4] Later he accepted Kim Dae Jung's invitation to join his personal foundation (the Kim Dae Jung Peace Foundation) as its secretary general and helped author Kim's 1995 book on Korean reunification. With Kim's election as president, Ambassador Lim was appointed senior secretary for National Security and Foreign Affairs at the Blue House, where he

---

[1]Kim Dae Jung, *The Korean Problem: Nuclear Crisis, Democracy, and Reunification* (Seoul: The Kim Dae Jung Peace Foundation, 1994).

[2]Kim Dae Jung, "Don't Take the Sunshine Away," *Korea and Asia: A Collection of Essays, Speeches, and Discussions* (Seoul: The Kim Dae Jung Peace Foundation, 1994), p. 33.

[3]Kim Dae Jung Peace Foundation, *Kim Dae Jung's Three Stage Approach to Korean Unification: Focusing on the South-North Confederal Stage* (Seoul: Asia-Pacific Peace Foundation Press, 1995).

[4]Lim served successively during this period as chancellor of the Institute for Foreign Affairs and National Security (IFANS), chairman of the Presidential Commission on Arms Control and delegate to the South-North Talks, and vice minister for Unification.

served as the principal architect of the sunshine policy and manager responsible for coordinating and managing its implementation. Thereafter he alternated between the Blue House and positions heading the National Intelligence Service (South Korea's CIA) and Ministry of Unification. In all positions, he exercised tight control over the planning, coordination, and implementation of policy toward North Korea.[5]

In assuming office, both men shared more than an aspiration for reconciliation with North Korea. They also shared remarkably similar worldviews. Both men agreed, for example, that the collapse of the Soviet Union, end of the Cold War, and widening gap in national power between Seoul and Pyongyang created an entirely new situation. They also agreed that North Korea would not collapse anytime soon, despite its severe economic conditions. On the contrary, they considered Pyongyang's economic straits as driving North Korea inexorably toward the "Chinese model" of reform and cooperation, while they saw in Kim Jong Il a reasonable leader willing to compromise—so long as his pride was maintained—and potential partner for peace. The task as they saw it was to show sincerity in seeking reconciliation, address North Korea's legitimate concerns, and provide Pyongyang a favorable environment in which it could opt for reform without feeling threatened.

Not surprisingly given these views, the two men were highly critical of the preceding Kim Young Sam administration. They saw their predecessors as having effectively given up the fruitful attempts at engagement begun by Roh Tae Woo and were particularly critical of their alleged policy flip-flops during the nuclear crisis. Acknowledging that their own views of North Korea diverged sharply from their predecessors, they were determined to fashion a more patient, consistent, and focused policy.

Under these two dominant figures, a handful of senior staff at the Ministry of Unification and National Intelligence Service has been influential in implementing policy. Their primary emphasis has

---

[5]In September 2001, Ambassador Lim was forced to resign as Minister of Unification when the National Assembly passed a vote of no confidence over the government's handling of a controversial visit of South Koreans to North Korea. He was subsequently made a "policy advisor" to the president in the Blue House.

.

been on identifying ways to make progress in North-South relations—that is, additional steps that can be taken to implement and advance the president's agenda. As in any modern state, a larger governmental apparatus supports the work of these key individuals.

The administration, to be sure, is not monolithic. A second loose school of thought exists within the administration that believes policy toward the North should be more "balanced" and place greater emphasis on North Korean reciprocity. This second school of thought, however, has no leader or organizational cohesion. It is simply a point of view held privately by a number of people within the administration.[6] Even if this were not the case, few have sufficient stature, or standing, to advocate an approach that is significantly different from that defined by the president and Ambassador Lim. In this sense, when people talk about "the government" or "the administration" in connection with the sunshine policy, they are talking overwhelmingly about the views or actions of these two individuals.

THE PARTIES

Political parties in Korea have traditionally been regarded as ciphers. They are organized around a single dominant personality. They lack political cohesion, institutionalized mechanisms, or even a core set of beliefs. They are also oriented almost exclusively to helping their leader get elected. Not surprisingly, they are often dismissed as insignificant policy actors. Korea's authoritarian tradition, coupled with the parties' own reliance on vague, equivocal policy statements, contributes to this general image. The political realities of the Kim Dae Jung administration, however, have given the parties roles to play in the debate over policy toward North Korea. Particularly important among these realities has been the ruling party's status as a minority party in the National Assembly, although the sharp societal divisions and larger process of democratization have also contributed.

---

[6]Dr. Ra Jong-il, a close advisor to President Kim in the first couple of years of the administration, was widely seen as one representative of this general school of thought. He is now serving as South Korea's ambassador to the United Kingdom.

The following are brief sketches of the three main parties and their general stances on the sunshine policy.

The Millennium Democratic Party (MDP)

The roots of President Kim's ruling party run back to the National Congress for New Politics (NCNP), which Kim formed in 1995 to run for president for the fourth time.[7] Kim transformed the NCNP into the MDP in January 2000 as part of a larger effort to refurbish the party's image, win the April 2000 legislative elections, and become the majority party in the National Assembly. Most MDP lawmakers are long-time followers of Kim Dae Jung.

As its origins and membership might suggest, the party has always been a major supporter of Kim's personal policy line.[8] The original party platform echoes Kim's call for dismantling the Cold War structure on the Korean Peninsula and establishing a foundation for unification; endorses the three basic principles of the government's sunshine policy; and urges expanded exchanges and cooperation with North Korea through a functionalist approach to North-South integration. The platform also emphasizes the "separation of economics and politics" principle as the means to foster economic cooperation and build a North-South economic community.[9]

Although the MDP muted its advocacy of the sunshine policy initially in an effort to avoid stirring up problems with South Korean conservatives, it stepped up its support after the June 2000 summit to reinforce the president's claim of major policy success. Arguing that the summit had put an end to the age of rivalry and hostility between the two Koreas, the party amended its platform to present itself more ag-

---

[7]Having resigned from his former party, the Peace and Democracy Party (PDP), following his loss to Kim Young Sam in the elections for president in December 1992, Kim formed the NCNP for his attempted comeback.

[8]Before the foundation of the MDP, the NCNP's policy was essentially a copy of that laid out in Kim Dae Jung's 1995 three-stage unification book. The platform renounced "unification by absorption" or "unification by force" and called for a gradual process of North-South reconciliation based on consensus, confidence building, and coexistence. National Congress for New Politics, *Party Platform* (Seoul: NCNP, 1997).

[9]New Millennium Democratic Party, *Party Platform, Constitutions and Regulations* (Seoul: MDP, 2000).

gressively as a political force able to initiate a new era of reconciliation, cooperation, and peaceful coexistence on the Korean Peninsula.[10]

The Grand National Party (GNP)

Like its MDP counterpart, the GNP is a product of substantial evolution. Unlike the MDP, it is a product of considerable cross-fertiliza-
tion. In 1990, Roh Tae Woo's ruling Democratic Justice Party (DJP)
merged with Kim Young Sam's Reunification Democratic Party
(RDP) and one other small opposition party to form the Democratic
Liberal Party (DLP). The DLP begot the New Korea Party (NKP) when
Kim Young Sam ran for president in 1992. Later the NKP merged
with the splinter opposition Democratic Party (DP) to form the GNP
when Lee Hoi Chang sought the presidency in 1997. Despite Lee's
loss in that year's election, the GNP has remained South Korea's
major opposition party, as well as the largest party in the National
Assembly. The GNP has also continued to be headed by Lee, who is
running for president again in the December 2002 elections.

Representing mainstream conservative forces in South Korean politics, the party has retained the three-step unification policy of the
Roh Tae Woo and Kim Young Sam administrations. While it has always supported dialogue with North Korea, it has opposed most aspects of the Kim Dae Jung government's approach. It has inveighed
in particular against "one-sided" concessions and warned loudly
against the "misuse" of the North-South summit for domestic political purposes. In general, the GNP has demanded a tougher stance
toward North Korea, including greater emphasis on "reciprocity,"
"verification" of North Korea's weapons of mass destruction, and the
end of "unidirectional" South Korean assistance to North Korea.

The United Liberal Democrats (ULD)

The ULD was formed in 1995 when Kim Jong-pil, the architect of
Park Chung Hee's military coup in 1961 and long-time ruling party
strongman, bolted the DLP and formed his own party. Outside of

---

[10]New Millennium Democratic Party, *Party Platform* (Seoul: MDP, August 2000).

Kim's personal and regional constituencies, the party's key supporters come from veterans' groups, anti-Communist organizations, and business firms—all of which, like Kim himself, are extremely conservative. Although generally regarded as even farther to the right than the GNP, the ULD formed an unholy alliance with Kim Dae Jung's MDP in order to win the 1997 presidential election.[11] In return for their participation in the ruling coalition, the ULD was given the prime minister's position and other cabinet seats, along with a promise that the MDP would agree to institute a parliamentary system of government—Kim Jong-pil's long-held goal—during the second half of President Kim's administration.

Kim Jong-pil is known to detest North Korea and strongly oppose the sunshine policy. While he supported the government up until the establishment of the MDP in January 2000, he sniped at and tried to slow down the sunshine policy incessantly from inside the government. The party's strong opposition to the sunshine policy emerged increasingly after the summit. President Kim's violation of his promise to move to a parliamentary system intensified the strife between the two coalition leaders. When a no confidence vote against sunshine policy architect Lim Dong-Won came up in the National Assembly in late 2001, Kim Jong-pil took his party out of the ruling coalition and voted with the opposition, forcing the resignation of Lim and the entire cabinet.

THE MILITARY

Democratization dealt a deathblow to the dominance of the military in South Korea. Aided by Roh Tae Woo's overt effort as president to distance himself from the military officers responsible for the December 1979 coup d'état and May 1980 Kwangjoo massacre, the military began in the late 1980s to assume a low profile. Still, expressions of military opposition to Roh's *"Nordpolitik"* and dialogue with North Korea were occasionally expressed, as when the commandant of the Korean Military Academy strongly criticized the government's

---

[11]One newspaper captured the broad party orientations succinctly: "The ULD is conservative and GNP is moderately conservative, while the MDP is progressive in relative terms." *JoongAng Ilbo*, February 2, 2002.

policy for having caused confusion in the military over who is South Korea's enemy.

In its attempt to carry democratization further and establish a fully civilian, democratic government, the Kim Young Sam administration further weakened the military's voice by uprooting the *Hanahoe* faction in the Korean Army. This highly politicized group of senior army officers had long dominated military leadership positions and still harbored hopes for a return by the military to its traditional position. By removing the generals in the *Hanahoe* from the military and abolishing the faction, Kim Young Sam also neutralized the group that had long oppressed Kim Dae Jung, inadvertently paving the way for him to subsequently become president.

Kim Jong-pil's decision to form a coalition with Kim Dae Jung helped mitigate traditional concerns within the military about the latter's ideological suitability for the presidency. One indication was the group of retired generals who publicly joined in supporting Kim's 1997 presidential campaign. This had the effect of dampening the impact of those active-duty and retired generals who opposed Kim's orientation on ideological grounds, while reinforcing the military's low profile. Lim Dong-Won's tight control over the participants and topics in National Security Council meetings further constrained the impact of military opposition to the government's policy, as did the government's screening process for the appointment of officers to senior command and leadership positions. There are reasons to believe that many in the military are very unhappy with the sunshine policy. They are particularly unhappy with what they see as the administration's priority, in practice, on engagement over security and its effort to reduce the Ministry of National Defense (MND) budget to help fund its sunshine activities. But they feel "sandwiched" and unable to express their opposition publicly.

Unlike their active-duty counterparts, many retired generals are more voluble in their opposition. The Korean Association of Retired Generals and Admirals, for example, often expresses the concerns of its members over the nature and speed of the government's approach to North Korea. A particular association criticism is that the government's policy has prematurely jettisoned North Korea as the ROK's enemy, weakening public support for national security in the process. This view appears to be widely shared among members of this group. One poll, for example, found that an absolute majority of retired generals and admirals still consider Pyongyang to be South Korea's enemy; in contrast, members of the government and government party were disinclined to identify North Korea in these terms.[12] Not surprisingly, retired generals and admirals rejected the notion of approaching North Korea in "one people" terms and welcomed the depiction of North Korea in the *Defense White Paper*—a document put out annually by MND until the government quashed its publication in 2001—as South Korea's continuing enemy. Other similar military organizations, such as the Korean Disabled Veterans Organization, are active in echoing these views. The high respect Koreans generally show for retired senior officers give such groups significant clout.

THE MEDIA

The major TV broadcasting companies, such as Korea Broadcasting System (KBS), Moonhwa Broadcasting Company (MBC), and Seoul Broadcasting System (SBS), have generally supported the sunshine policy, reflecting in part perhaps the high degree of government control over the broadcasting industry. The major newspapers, on the other hand, have been sharply divided. Mirroring the broader ideological division in South Korean society, progressive papers have been strongly supportive of the sunshine policy. The *Hankyoreh Sinmun*, a newspaper closely associated with South Korea's radical left, is particularly influential in progressive circles. The conservative papers take highly critical, although somewhat more nuanced, positions. Newspapers like the *JoongAng Ilbo* mix mild support for the principle of engagement with criticism of the way the government has fashioned and implemented its policy. The *Chosun Ilbo, Donga Ilbo*, and *Kookmin Ilbo* are strident critics. Coincidentally or otherwise, the unprecedented government attack on the media in the summer of 2001 under the rubric of "reforming the press" was focused on this latter group of newspapers.[13]

---

[12]Kyong-Mann Jeon, Ju-Suk Suh, Gosson Dok, and Bum-Chul Shin, *Survey on Security Environment After the South-North Summit Meeting* (Seoul: Korea Institute for Defense Analyses, December 2000).

[13]The conservative press has *never* supported Kim Dae Jung throughout the past 40 years, and the hostility is fully reciprocated. Participants on both sides of the relation-

The administration's attack indirectly highlights another feature of the press in South Korea: its highly influential position. While the press is important in all democratic societies, it is somewhat unique in Korea in two respects. First, it has existed longer than the country itself. Whereas the ROK was established only in 1948, the major newspapers have existed since the 1920s. Second, much of Korea's political elite rose through journalism. This was the only option open to politically attuned South Koreans during the Japanese colonial period, and it remained an esteemed career throughout the postwar decades of dictatorial rule. In the process, the press came to see itself not as observers, or even watchdogs, of the political process but rather as direct participants. Not surprisingly, many former newsmen, especially media figures, wind up being elected to the National Assembly. These unique features have reinforced, if not exacerbated, the sharp ideological and other divisions in South Korea, while posing obstacles not only to the administration's North Korea policy but also to its larger domestic political objectives.

One other factor contributes to the particular importance of the press: the general weakness of political parties. As noted above, most political parties are aggregations of disparate groups held together by loyalty to a particular leader. For this reason, they are seen more as political lackeys than important articulators of public policy. Newspapers have stepped in to fill the vacuum, with the *Chosun Ilbo* on the right and *Hankyoreh Sinmun* on the left serving effectively as goal posts around which the conservative and progressive camps, respectively, gather. In a country as highly literate as South Korea, where virtually everyone reads one or another of the major national dailies, this gives them enormous influence.

The following are thumbnail sketches of the four major newspapers.

Chosun Ilbo

The *Chosun Ilbo*, established in 1920, is both the oldest and largest (in terms of circulation) newspaper in Korea today. The founder of the paper originally came from North Korea, and he and his succes-

---

ship describe a situation of open warfare, with each side focused on strengthening its respective base of power in what is candidly described as attempts to undermine—if not destroy—the other as a political force.

sors (the current head is the founder's grandson) are stridently anti-Communist in their political orientation. As an open supporter of Kim Young Sam in the 1992 presidential election, the paper maintained a friendly relationship with the government throughout that administration.[14] Its deep, decades-long, ideology-based antagonism to Kim Dae Jung and strong support of GNP candidate Lee Hoi Chang in the 1997 election, on the other hand, ensured a tense relationship with the Kim Dae Jung administration from the outset.

The paper's drumbeat of harsh criticisms of President Kim's approach toward North Korea made relations worse. While the paper has taken the administration to task for many things, it has particularly criticized its approach for having weakened South Korea's security, while predicating South Korean policy on the "naïve" assumption that North Korea can be enticed to change. It also has denounced government officials for having woefully misread North Korea's intentions, thereby allowing the government to be bullied by North Koreans without any recourse. Arguing that North Korea has abused South Korea's goodwill while continuing its provocations, the paper has called for a policy focused on strengthening South Korea's deterrent capabilities and rigorously applying the rule of reciprocity in all North-South interactions.[15]

Donga Ilbo

The nearly equally venerable *Donga Ilbo* had a very large circulation until the 1980s. During that decade, Chun Doo Hwan cracked down hard on the paper for vigorously protesting (including through the use of blank advertisements) the regime's restrictions on freedom of the press. Readership fell thereafter. The *Donga Ilbo* from the beginning has questioned the efficacy of the sunshine policy, as well as many of its underlying assumptions. It has also criticized the administration's alleged timidity in dealing with North Korea, citing its re-

---

[14]Hong Won Park, *North Korea Policy and Relationship Between the Press and the State: Comparative Analysis on the Contents of Chosun Ilbo and Hankyoreh Sinmun* (Seoul: The Korea Press Foundation, 2001), p. 32.

[15]*Chosun Ilbo*, June 24, 1998. North Korea has reciprocated in kind, banning *Chosun Ilbo* reporters from participating in trips to the North and targeting severe propaganda attacks on, and threats against, the newspaper company.

luctance to raise human rights issues with the North or insist that humanitarian issues high on South Korea's agenda be linked to food assistance or other issues important to North Korea. The paper has expressed strong doubts about the sincerity of Kim Jong Il's reputed statement that he accepts the U.S. military presence in South Korea, while it has warned against revising South Korea's National Security Law until there is evidence of a corresponding change in Pyongyang's attitude.

JoongAng Ilbo

Despite its relatively recent establishment in 1965, the *JoongAng Ilbo* now has the second largest circulation of South Korean newspapers. Of the main conservative press, it has been the most moderate and balanced in its criticisms of the sunshine policy, striving strenuously to evaluate the policy on an issue-by-issue basis. The paper has supported the sunshine policy's broad goal of engaging North Korea, for example, predicated on the practical view that South Korea's best option given current conditions is to keep North Korea essentially as it is. The paper has criticized the administration, however, for the speed with which it has moved to improve relations with North Korea, the personalization of the North-South relationship, and the lack of transparency in the policymaking process. It also has criticized the administration for giving away too much to the North for too little in return and insisted that reciprocity should be applied to all interactions between the two Koreas.

Among other things, the *JoongAng Ilbo* was the first paper to publish a criticism of the absence of any reference in the summit's Joint Statement to reducing tensions and building a structure of peace on the Korean Peninsula. Since the summit, and with the warfare between the government and its critics in the press, the paper has stepped up its criticism of the sunshine policy, reflecting the difficulty of maintaining a relatively balanced viewpoint in an increasingly "black and white" atmosphere.

Hankyoreh Sinmun

The *Hankyoreh Sinmun* has no difficulty with the government's attack on the other major papers. Founded in 1987 as a product of the citizen's movements against South Korea's military dictatorship and partaking of their same "class-based" orientation, it does not regard these newspapers as "legitimate" representatives of the Korean people.[16] Not surprisingly, the *Hankyoreh* endorsed Kim Dae Jung in both the 1992 and 1997 presidential elections as the candidate closest to its own ideology.[17] Since Kim became president, the paper has supported his government across the board. It has been supportive of the sunshine policy in particular based on a relatively simple point of view: Koreans are "one people"; it is therefore incumbent on South Koreans to do everything they can to aid the North and promote unification. Seeing North Korea as a partner in cooperation, the *Hankyoreh* regards the sunshine policy as a means for reducing the possibility of war and fostering inter-Korean reconciliation. It also agrees with one of the critical assumptions underlying the policy: In order to open up and induce change in North Korea, there is no alternative to the approach followed by the government.[18]

CIVIC GROUPS AND NONGOVERNMENTAL ORGANIZATIONS

Civil society groups in South Korea are not unique. Like their counterparts elsewhere, many share a different ideological vision from that held by the traditionally dominant power groups and seek to force a new set of issues onto a public agenda from which they have been excluded. These groups have been particularly significant in South Korea, however, for at least three reasons. First, they filled a gap left by decades of dictatorial rule and are heavily colored, in turn, by the nature of their experience during that period.[19] Second, they

---

[16]Progressive groups characterize the major newspaper companies as "slaves" of their owners. Lumping them together with doctors, private school owners, and several other professional groups they consider "thieves" ripping off the unsuspecting masses, these groups see the government's attack on the media not as a "freedom of the press" issue but as a "moral issue" of right and wrong.

[17]Hong Won Park, op. cit., p. 32.

[18]*Hankyoreh Sinmun*, June 17, 1999.

[19]Although a strong civil society goes back as far as the Japanese colonial period, the contemporary phenomenon is really a product of the democratization movement—most directly the massive demonstrations of June 1987 and then-ruling party Chairman Roh Tae Woo's subsequent agreement to allow the direct election of the president. This experience influences everything from the goals to the leadership of many

have grown astronomically, with literally thousands of South Korean civic groups and NGOs having emerged in the last few years alone.[20] Third, they cast a broad net in defining their interests, with many groups participating in nationwide coalitions and other cooperative activities that advance broadly shared goals but go well beyond their more focused organizational mission.[21]

Using highly motivated volunteers and a variety of innovative methods, these groups are now contending against other South Korean power groups in almost all sectors. Active government support undoubtedly contributed to this development. The "Law to Support Non-profit Civic Organizations" adopted by the Kim Dae Jung administration has been particularly important in this regard, funneling 15 billion won annually to national and local NGOs.[22]

Contemporary civic groups and NGOs may be categorized in different ways. Many Koreans, for example, talk of these groups in terms of the broad social movement from which they emerged. Examples include the radical student and people's democratization movement (which includes highly ideological, class-conscious groups such as the Korean Association of Students and the Alliance for Democratic Unification and People's Movement); the more moderate but still reform-oriented citizens' movement (which includes groups like the Citizens' Coalition for Economic Justice); the occupation-based social movement emerging from the fierce labor struggles of the late 1980s (which includes groups like the Korea Trade Union Congress,

of these organizations. For details on the historical development of civil society groups in different periods, see Sunhyuk Kim, *Politics of Democratization in Korea: The Role of Civil Society* (University of Pittsburgh Press, 2000).

[20]Sungsoo Joo, "Understanding the NGO Revolution in Korea," an unpublished paper presented at the International Nonprofit Organization Conference "Northeast Asia Civil Society: Current Status and Challenging Roles of NGOs in Korea, Japan and China," November 11, 2000, Institute of East and West Studies, Yonsei University, Seoul, Korea.

[21]One example is the hundreds of diverse groups that joined forces in the Citizens' Alliance for the 2000 General Elections (CAGE) to defeat allegedly corrupt or incompetent politicians in the April 2000 National Assembly elections. For a useful account, see Andrew Eungi Kim, "Citizens' Coalition Movement and Consolidation of Democracy: 2000 General Elections in South Korea," *Journal of East Asian Studies*, Vol. 1, No. 2, August 2001.

[22]Keunjoo Lee, *Support for NGOs and the Government* (*NGO Jiwon kwa Jungbu*) (Seoul: Korea Institute of Government, 2000), p. 20.

Korea Teachers Union, and Korean Farmers' Movement Coalition); and the traditional conservative social movement (which includes groups long supported by South Korea's authoritarian governments like the New Village Movement and the Korean Anti-Communism League). Other Koreans categorize the groups in terms of their principal goal or focus of interest. These include anti-U.S. military base groups, environmental groups, and other issue-oriented groupings.

In terms of unification and inter-Korean issues, however, such groups may generally be divided simply into "progressive" and "conservative" categories. This reflects in part the ideological quotient of these issues in South Korea. It also reflects an artifact of history: Until the 1990s, a combination of government repression and social taboo made "reunification" issues almost exclusively the province of the radical student and people's movement—outside of the government and handful of conservative civic organizations it controlled. Even today, despite an effort to broaden participation, leadership of the major civic groups and NGOs active on unification issues remains largely in the hands of individuals who were deeply involved in the student and radical reunification movement. This contributed to the sharp polarization of positions and personalities on almost all of these issues.

The following are brief overviews of the major civic groups and NGOs active on policy toward North Korea on the "progressive" side of the spectrum.

Korean Council for Reconciliation and Cooperation (KCRC)

The KCRC, an umbrella organization open to all political parties and social groups interested in North-South reconciliation, was established in August 1998. Membership includes the MDP, ULD, 32 unification-related groups, 42 civic groups, and a wide range of others. The Kim Dae Jung administration had two goals in encouraging the KCRC's establishment: to actively promote inter-Korean exchanges and cooperation on a nongovernmental level; and to co-opt, or at least restrain, conservative groups opposed to the government's policy.[23] The hope was to thereby build greater support in South Korea for expanded cooperation and exchanges with North Korea as a means to promote inter-Korean reconciliation. The KCRC has accordingly strongly supported the government's policy, giving heavy emphasis to implementing the North-South "Basic Agreement" of 1991 in particular.[24] It also has stressed the importance of "people exchange," sending numerous delegations to the North and encouraging support for the Mt. Kumgang tourist project despite its financial nonviability.

Two problems have hindered the KCRC's efforts. First, despite its all-inclusive orientation, it has failed to involve the GNP, the Korea Veterans Association, and other major conservative civic groups in its membership and activities. Second, although the KCRC talks about the importance of facilitating dialogue and understanding among South Koreans as a means for building greater domestic consensus ("South-South dialogue"), in practice it has given far greater priority to promoting activities with North Korea ("South-North dialogue"). Both problems may be related to an underlying organizational difficulty: Leadership at key levels is in the hands of people long involved in the radical reunification movement. As a result, even activists in the NGO movement acknowledge that the KCRC is being used more to promote the strategic goals of the radical left than to co-opt or appeal to the conservative right. Still, it is a significant political force pushing for expanded interactions with North Korea.

Citizen's Coalition for Economic Justice (CCEJ)

Outside of the KCRC, the CCEJ is the most important umbrella group dealing with policy toward North Korea. As its title implies, the CCEJ's primary focus since its establishment in 1989 is on promoting

---

[23]North Korea has long proposed meetings among all Korean political parties and social groups—under the guise of forging a "grand national integration"—as a means for circumventing direct government-to-government talks and undermining the South Korean government. Previous South Korean governments had equally long rejected these proposals. President Kim supported a different approach, however, seeing expanded nongovernmental interactions as both a boost to his sunshine policy and a means for neutralizing some of its opponents. The KCRC was one result.

[24]Korean Council for Reconciliation and Cooperation, *For Unification and the Future with KCRC* (Seoul: KCRC, 1998).

economic justice in South Korean society.[25] Its efforts in this area span a broad range of notable, nonpolitical activities. The CCEJ also has a reunification committee, however, which is charged with mobilizing support for engagement with North Korea and promoting unification. This committee, founded in 1994, promotes expanded inter-Korean cooperation.

Although the CCEJ shares the "one Korea" orientation of most South Korean progressives, it split with the then head of the reunification committee over the question of whether to participate in North Korea's August 15, 2001, celebrations commemorating Korea's liberation from Japan. Seeing this trip (correctly as it turned out) as being too "political" and supportive of North Korea's agenda, the CCEJ opposed participation, which led to the resignation of the reunification committee's head. This tiff reflects broader, if incipient, tensions beginning to emerge between the most and less radical of the left. The CCEJ is currently focused more on preserving the gains made by the sunshine policy against conservative attacks than on moving in any major new direction.

People's Solidarity for Participatory Democracy (PSPD)

The PSPD was founded in 1994 with the aim of building a participatory, democratic society in which freedom, justice, human rights, and welfare are realized in South Korea. A nonpartisan, "network" kind of organization combining various roles played in the United States by the ACLU, American Bar Association, and Common Cause (among others), the PSPD monitors the government, National Assembly, and judiciary through an extensive array of voluntary citizens' committees. It not only proposes policy alternatives to different government bodies, it also drafts its own legislation (e.g., an anticorruption law, a social welfare law, a tenant rights bill, etc.), approximately half of which are adopted.

The PSPD does not have a dedicated staff for unification issues. However, it endorses the sunshine policy and actively helps mobilize support on the government's behalf. If anything, the PSPD feels the

---

[25]Citizen's Coalition for Economic Justice, *Documents to Commemorate the First Anniversary of the Coalition* (Seoul: CCEJ, 1990), p. 9.

administration has not moved far or fast enough to improve relations with North Korea. It is critical of what it considers a number of administration "mistakes" that have bolstered conservatives and set back the reform agenda. The PSPD's growing success and reputation for integrity give it significant exposure in the mass media, through which it seeks to influence public opinion.[26] Only seven years after its establishment, the PSPD became one of the largest NGOs in South Korea.

Anti-U.S. and Anti-U.S. Military Base NGOs

As a general statement, most of these groups can be considered part of the larger progressive (pro-peace/democracy/unification) movement. Although they do not focus primarily on North-South issues, they generally share the views (e.g., Koreans are all "one people," North Korea is not an enemy, etc.) of those who do. More importantly, they increasingly see a linkage between U.S. policies on security issues and the state of North-South relations. Many insist, for example, that North Korea has stalled the North-South dialogue only because of the "hard-line" U.S. stance toward North Korea. Some believe that the United States is at the heart of all of Korea's problems. They thus conduct organized protests not only against the U.S. military presence in Korea but against the Status of Forces Agreement (SOFA), missile defense program, and U.S. security policies more broadly.

Many of these groups believe that the ultimate key to peace and unification—as well as to ending the U.S. military presence and "unequal" U.S.-ROK relationship—is fostering North-South reconciliation and ending the division of the peninsula. They actively participate in missions to North Korea, therefore, as well as in other civic group efforts to promote North-South relations. Representative groups include Solidarity for Peace and Reunification of Korea, National Campaign for Eradication of Crime by US Troops in Korea, Solidarity for Revision of SOFA, Committee for Joint Measures to Stop US Missile Defense and to Realize Peace, and National Alliance for Democracy and Unification of Korea.

---

[26]Kyungran Moon, *We Have a Dream* (*Uriegeneun Kkumi Issseumnida*) (Seoul: Nanam Publisher, 2000).

Labor Groups

South Korea's two major labor groups, the Federation of Korean Trade Unions (FKTU) and the Korean Confederation of Trade Unions (KCTU), share many of the characteristics described above (although the latter is closer to the other progressive NGOs because of its development as an independent organization). Both are advocates of the "one Korea" position. Both believe the key to peace and prosperity is promoting cooperation with North Korea. And both strongly support the administration's sunshine policy as the only realistic policy. Although they do not focus on North-South issues, they actively participate in delegations to North Korea to emphasize "solidarity" with North Korean workers. They also participate in activities organized by other civic groups, including protests against U.S. policy toward North Korea. While not major actors themselves, they contribute to the nature and intensity of debate over policies toward North Korea.

On the conservative side of the spectrum, social groups did not really begin forming as genuine NGOs until the Kim Young Sam administration. As the recipients of direct and exclusive government support, they saw little need before then. The general conservatism of Korean society may have further delayed adaptation to the new internal and external environments by creating something of a false sense of security. In contrast to the situation in the West, however, Korean conservatism suffers from a key weakness. Largely lacking philosophical and religious foundations, it is heavily dependent for its public appeal on the perceived need to strengthen the ruling establishment through "anti-Communism."[27] With the collapse of the Soviet Union and economic free-fall of North Korea, this appeal greatly diminished.

The advent of civilian democratic government in South Korea and demand for broad societal reforms, however, gradually made these groups aware that they needed to change if they were to survive on their own. The rise of the "pure" NGOs (i.e., "progressive" groups that had not been adjuncts of the military regimes) in the mid-1990s

---

[27]Yong Min Kim, "Origin and Evolution of Western Conservatism" (*Seoku Bosujuui ui Kiwon kwa Baljun*), in Byung Kook Kim et al., eds., *Korea's Conservatism* (*Hankuk ui BosuJuui*), (Seoul: Ingansarang Publisher, 1999), p. 47.

reinforced this message. In response, conservative groups began to emphasize liberal democracy and an open market economy as their organizational rationale and means for garnering public favor. The civic groups and NGOs on the conservative side most active on North Korean issues include the following.

National Congress of Freedom and Democracy (NCFD)

The NCFD was organized in 1994 as a coalition of 33 conservative civic groups, such as the Korean Freedom League, the Daehan Anti-Communist Youths, and the National Building Youth Council, to promote conservative views on security and unification issues. The head of the NCFD is Lee Chul Seung, a prominent opposition leader during the 1970s.

In the face of charges that the NCFD is "ultra-conservative" and stuck with a "Cold War mentality," Lee has argued that the organization is the representative of South Korea's "true progressives," since it alone seeks to protect and preserve the country's liberal democracy. The NCFD opposes the sunshine policy for many reasons. It is particularly critical of the policy's emphasis on promoting Korea's "self-reliant" unification, which it feels is inappropriate and dangerous in the absence of prior efforts to build military confidence and reduce the danger of war on the Korean peninsula.[28] The NCFD also has been outspoken in opposing a visit by Kim Jong Il to Seoul. It insists on a formal apology first for North Korea's past terrorist activities and a pledge to end its weapons of mass destruction program, missile activity, and other threatening behavior.

Korean Freedom League (KFL)

The KFL came into being in 1989 as the transformed version of the Korean Anti-Communism League, which was founded originally in 1964. Both organizations supported government actions to suppress pro-Communist actions. In an effort to broaden its appeal following the collapse of Communist regimes in the world and the end of the

---

[28]Sung Won Park, "Conservatives Looking for Counterattack by the Progressives" (*Bosu neun Bangyok eul Norinda*), *Shindonga*, September 2000, pp. 76–109.

Cold War, however, the KFL created a new platform giving greater emphasis to protecting freedom and liberal democracy. Accordingly, it has stressed the inherent connection between peace and freedom and criticized the administration harshly for ignoring the plight of the North Korean people. As a leading member of the NCFD, the KFL subscribes to most of its positions. It has also been active independently in supporting the U.S. military presence and the U.S.-ROK security alliance.

Korean Veterans Association (KVA)

As one of the oldest groups in Korea, the Korean Veterans Association played a major role supporting South Korean military governments until the 1980s. During this period, the association and the former Anti-Communism League would mobilize their members for large demonstrations in support of the government whenever North Korea committed one of its numerous provocations. Since the June 2000 summit, however, the association has had difficulty balancing between its historic support of the government in power and its traditional conservative position on policy issues. The result has been a compromise: The association supports the sunshine policy in principle while it distances itself from aspects of the policy it does not like.

One example of the latter is the failure of the government to address the issue of South Korean prisoners of war held by Pyongyang since the Korean War, particularly given the administration's decision to unilaterally return North Korean prisoners held in South Korean jails to the North. Another is the administration's "unidirectional" assistance, which the KVA sees as producing little in return and symptomatic of a broader administration weakness in dealing with North Korea.[29] The association is highly critical of the government's decision to allow South Korean delegates to participate in North Korea's August 2001 "Liberation Day" celebrations, which it sees as weakening South Korea's will to defend itself.

---

[29]Ibid., p. 84.

THE PRIVATE SECTOR

As a general statement, the South Korean private sector is cautious and risk averse when it comes to dealings with North Korea. This stems from worries that economic interactions will require large initial investments and a long period of time before they become profitable, if ever. Many if not most of those in the private sector agree on the need to provide humanitarian assistance to the North. But they approach the North more in conservative, profit-oriented terms than in terms of nationalism or emotional, "one-people" images. Given this orientation, they tend to see China and even Vietnam as better business partners, although they are interested in low-level explorations of potential economic ventures in the North pending longer-term changes.

Two business organizations have been active in trying to foster North-South interactions: the Federation of Korean Industries (FKI), representing big business, and the Korea Federation of Small Business (KFSB), representing small business interests. Both have sent investment teams to the North to explore possibilities for promoting inter-Korean economic cooperation. Neither has been very optimistic. Although they have developed a range of potential investment plans, most South Korean businessmen have seen little of the kind of change in the North necessary to support large-scale investment assistance. The experiences of Hyundai in the Mt. Kumgang and other investment projects have reinforced this general orientation. Initial mixed feelings about the Hyundai initiatives—if they succeeded, after all, Hyundai would reap all the benefits—have largely been replaced by relief over their own caution.[30] Reluctant to

---

[30]The Mt. Kumgang project failed not only because Hyundai miscalculated the number of South Korean tourists who would participate but also because North Korea did not open up inland routes to the scenic tourist area, which would have facilitated travel and relieved Hyundai's operating expenses. As a result, the Hyundai Asan Group managing the project went bankrupt. In the middle of its own restructuring, the parent Hyundai conglomerate could not absorb Hyundai Asan's debt and the Mt. Kumgang project was cast adrift. As of June 2001, the Hyundai Asan Group owed the North $24 million. On June 8, the two sides reached agreement to have Hyundai pay $12 million plus $100 per traveler. The Korea National Tourism Organization (KNTO), a South Korean government-sponsored agency, then stepped in to take charge of the Mt. Kumgang project as a way to bail out the Hyundai Asan Group. With this support, the Hyundai Asan Group cleared its remaining debt to the North in March 2002.

get too involved in interactions with North Korea, most businesses have focused their efforts on trying to resist government pressure.

There appear to be few major differences between large and small business in their attitudes toward the sunshine policy. In general, both support the principle of engagement with North Korea and, hence, the basic impulse of the sunshine policy. They are critical of the way this policy has been implemented however. They are particularly critical of the administration's haste in trying to expedite expanded interactions, as well as the short shrift they believe the administration has given to the importance of consensus building in South Korea. Both tendencies, in their view, exacerbated the divisions within South Korean society. They also hindered provision of government funds for inter-Korean cooperation, while inducing the National Assembly to reject a number of North-South agreements critical to expanded economic interactions.

South Korean businessmen generally agree that a return visit by Kim Jong Il to Seoul is a prerequisite for any revitalization of North-South economic activity, because they believe that he alone will be able to induce the kinds of changes inside the North that will make this possible. Few are making plans based on any of this happening any time soon.[31]

PUBLIC OPINION

Public opinion as a major factor influencing South Korean policies toward North Korea is a relatively new phenomenon, as described in Chapter Two. Not surprisingly, numerous polls are conducted to measure this new phenomenon. The Ministry of Unification conducts polls on issues dealing with policy toward North Korea at least

---

[31]The Northeast Asia Economy Center of the Federation of Korean Industries, *Status and Implications of South-North Economic Cooperation of Major Enterprises* (Seoul: FKI CEM 2001-22, 2001). This report is based on surveys taken of 600 large firms in South Korea, asking their views on a range of issues affecting North-South economic cooperation. Among other interesting findings: Eighty-eight percent of the firms indicated they are not currently planning to pursue projects with North Korea in the future. Sixty-one percent said that social infrastructure in the North would have to be significantly improved before initiatives like the pending Kaesong Industrial Complex project could succeed. And 77 percent said that a return visit by Kim Jong Il to Seoul is essential to reactivate inter-Korean economic cooperation.

two to three times a year. The major newspapers conduct their own polls regularly as well, sometimes independently and sometimes with Gallup Korea. Despite the number and frequency of these polls, acquiring a clear understanding of the nature of public opinion is difficult for a variety of reasons. These range from the incomparability of survey instruments and patently tendentious or simplistic questionnaires to the questionable competence, and accountability, of some of the firms doing the polling. The safest way to proceed is to assume that virtually all publicly released polls are distorted in one way or another.[32]

At a general level, however, the polls support at least three broad statements:

- First, the June 2000 summit was a break point in public opinion. Before the summit, the rate of public support for the sunshine policy was both relatively high (reaching 80–94 percent on the eve of the summit) and relatively consistent across the polls; thereafter, the support rate declined significantly as time passed in almost all polls other than those of the government.[33]

- Second, public opinion shows sharp divisions on many issues. Forty-six percent of the public might say in one poll, for example, that they believe the government's policy has been well implemented while another 46 percent will say it has not been well implemented. Forty percent in another poll might say they believe liberal democracy is the best system for a unified Korea, while 37 percent will express a preference for a mixed system that includes aspects of the North's Communist system.

---

[32]This certainly is the way the main protagonists proceed in Korea itself. The government interprets the polls taken by the major media groups as reflecting their hostile views toward the government and negative attitudes toward its sunshine policy. Most everyone else discounts the government polls as designed to support the government's North Korea and domestic policy objectives.

[33]The falloff in support was particularly acute in a survey conducted by Gallup Korea and the *Chosun Ilbo*: Whereas nearly 87 percent of the respondents supported the sunshine policy in August 2000, this number fell to 49 percent in February 2001 and then to only 34 percent in June 2001. *Chosun Ilbo*, August 24, 2000 and Gallup Korea web site, http://egallup31.gallup.co.kr/News/. The government's polls, in contrast, consistently register public support at more than 60 percent.

- Third, attitudes toward the government's policy are affected by South Korea's persistent problem of regionalism. The rates of support for the sunshine policy from those in President Kim's home Cholla provinces, for example, consistently are 20–30 percent higher than the comparable rates for those from the Kyongsang provinces, the home regions of most of South Korea's previous presidents.[34]

Whatever the precise nature of public opinion at any particular moment, it is clear that public opinion matters. Not only has President Kim's administration taken polls far more frequently than any previous South Korean government, it has actively used these government surveys to justify and accelerate its engagement efforts. The story of the sunshine policy is, to an important degree, the story of changes over time in public opinion.

ENVIRONMENTAL MAPPING: A NOTIONAL MATRIX

Although most Koreans support some kind of effort to engage North Korea, the major South Korean actors, as the brief accounts above suggest, are sharply divided between supporters and opponents of the sunshine policy. They are equally divided on the effectiveness of the policy in producing changes in North Korea. Figure 1 provides a notional depiction of where the major groups fall on these two issues.

This notional matrix shows a sharply bipolar distribution, with a relatively small number of actors in the "middle." If anything, it understates the divide. As suggested above, for example, many in the

---

[34]The largest regional gaps tend to be when the rate of support declines sharply. Jun Han, "Change in the Public Perception of North Korea, Unification, and North-South Relations After the Inter-Korean Summit," *Social Criticism Quarterly* (*Kyegan Sahoe Bipyong*), Summer 2001, pp. 247–261. On the "has policy been well implemented" question, for example, a December 2000 poll showed that nearly 80 percent of the people in the Cholla provinces answered affirmatively (versus only 10 percent who said policy had not been well implemented). In contrast, only 34 percent and 40 percent of the people in the two Kyongsang provinces thought the policy had been well implemented (versus 57 percent and 46 percent who thought the opposite). Gallup Korea web site, op. cit.

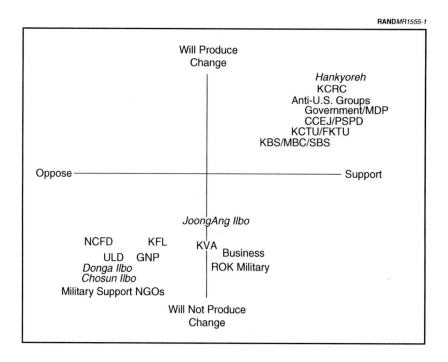

RAND*MR1555-1*

Figure 1—Notional Positions of Major Actors on Sunshine Policy

ROK military do not personally support the sunshine policy, although the military as an institution has shown moderate support. Similarly, while most business groups express support for the government's policy, many are critical of important aspects of its handling of relations with the North. Also, even among many policy supporters, there is very little expectation that the administration's approach will succeed in producing significant change inside North Korea.

This divide was not nearly as pronounced at the beginning of the Kim Dae Jung administration. As indicated in Chapter Two, there was in fact a growing consensus in South Korea in favor of efforts to engage North Korea, a consensus that bolstered proponents of the sunshine policy and provided a basis on which to build. What happened to change this situation is the subject of the next chapter.

Chapter Six

INTERNAL DYNAMICS: THE PROCESS

The process through which a major debate often moves is much like a calendar: Each has its seasons. The watershed event in the sunshine policy's cycle was clearly the June 2000 summit. This event transformed what had been a relatively low-level public discourse into a major public brouhaha. But two other events had significant effects on the internal dynamics as well and contributed directly to the debate's nature and direction. One was President Kim's decision in January 2000 to form a new political party. This decision, understandable given the president's political position and policy aspirations, politicized what had been generally considered until then a nonpartisan issue. In the process, it riled relations within the ruling coalition and exacerbated the task of generating broader public consensus behind the administration's policies. The other was the inauguration of George W. Bush as president of the United States in January 2001. The advent of the Bush administration gave North Korea an excuse to delay dialogue with South Korea (as well as with the United States), while the public articulation of the Bush administration's new approach—as filtered through the South Korean media—further fueled a domestic debate that was already raging.

These events serve as benchmarks for the debate's seasons. The period between President Kim's inauguration in February 1998 and his decision to form a new party in January 2000 might be thought of as the "spring" of the debate. During this period, general support for the idea of trying to engage North Korea, along with continued North Korean rigidity and the exigencies of Korea's severe financial crisis, made public debate desultory, while seeds were quietly being planted for new growth later in the "year." The period between January 2000, when President Kim formed his new party, and the June 2000 summit was a short but intense "summer." This period saw a series of sizzling developments, along with their concomitant dark clouds and sudden summer storms. Period three, from the summit to the beginning of the Bush administration, was the "fall," with intense efforts by one side in the debate to harvest the fruits of the summer's growth countered by equally intense efforts by the other side to frustrate and counter these efforts. "Winter" came in the fourth period, from January 2001 to October 2002. Appropriately long for South Korea's harsh political climate, this period saw a freeze in North-South relations, solidification of the divides in South Korean politics, and a growing chill in U.S.-ROK relations. This chapter describes how this all happened.

SPRING (FEBRUARY 1998 TO JANUARY 2000)

As described in Chapter Three, President Kim came into office fully determined to pursue his commitment to engagement. He made this clear in his inaugural address when he said that reconciliation and cooperation with the North would be a top priority of his administration despite Pyongyang's continuing bellicosity and the severe financial crisis that had just hit South Korea. Kim was not only determined but also confident. His decades as a major national figure and years of thinking about unification issues convinced him that he understood North Korea better, and could accomplish more, than his predecessors, who he believed had exaggerated the North Korean threat and failed to approach North Korea with the proper sensitivity and understanding.

With this confidence and determination, the administration described the goal of its policy as being to improve North-South relations as a means for inducing change inside North Korea and thereby hastening reconciliation. To President Kim and the key people in his government, this meant providing North Korea a favorable environment in which it could opt for openness and reform without feeling threatened. Providing such an environment, however, is difficult in the best of circumstances given the deep distrust of the North in South Korea—not to mention North Korea's own paranoia, erratic behavior, and inherent vulnerability. At a minimum, sustained domestic support is required to allow sufficient time to demonstrate the policy's success.

Beyond this requirement, President Kim faced several additional impediments to rapid forward movement when he first came to power:

- The "odd couple" coalition he formed with Kim Jong-pil to secure his election brought South Korea's ideological divide directly into his administration, creating significant constraints on how fast he could move in implementing his policy.

- The minority status of Kim's party in the National Assembly prevented it from unilaterally passing budgets and other legislation needed to help North Korea, increasing the president's reliance on the ruling coalition and the time and energy required to achieve compromise.

- The economy, reeling from the Asian financial crisis that hit South Korea in late 1997, was in no position to churn up large amounts of assistance for North Korea, simultaneously preoccupying the president and reinforcing the need for a "go-it-slow" approach.

- President Kim himself was deeply distrusted by large segments of the South Korean population because of his alleged "leftist" leanings, which bolstered the need for moderation in pursuing his policy objectives.

Reflecting awareness of these constraints, Kim moved cautiously at first. He emphasized that deterrence and reconciliation with the North would be pursued simultaneously. He stressed rhetorically the need for domestic consensus. He also promised that his approach to Pyongyang would be open and transparent. In addition, President Kim gave key government security posts to well-known conservative heavyweights, such as Kang In-duk (Minister of Unification) and Lee Jong Chan (director of the National Intelligence Agency), in an effort to mitigate widespread suspicions about his ideological affinities. As a further sop to conservatives, he allowed his Minister of Unification to announce that engagement would be pursued only on the basis of strict reciprocity. All this was designed to reassure a suspicious public and buy time for his sunshine policy to work.

At the same time, however, the president was beginning to move forward. In February 1998, he publicly ruled out any South Korean efforts to undermine or absorb the North and pledged active efforts to promote inter-Korean reconciliation. In March, the government announced the principle of separating economics from politics in order to create a more favorable environment for the resumption of inter-Korean relations. In April, it promised to simplify legal procedures for inter-Korean business interactions, ultimately lifting ceilings on South Korean investment in the North. Shortly thereafter President Kim authorized the Hyundai Group to donate 1,000 head of cattle to the North to facilitate efforts by its chairman, Chung Ju-yung, to establish tourist and investment activities in North Korea. To assure smooth implementation of his sunshine policy, moreover, he delegated authority to Ambassador Lim Dong-Won, then National Security advisor at the Blue House, to appoint the senior members of the National Security Council and supervise the activities of anyone involved in policy toward North Korea.

An early fruit of these efforts appeared in November 1998 when a luxury cruise ship carrying about 900 South Korean tourists set sail for North Korea's scenic Mt. Kumgang. This historic trip marked the first time that any South Korean legally entered the North as a tourist since the two governments were established 50 years earlier.[1]

Unfortunately for President Kim and his sunshine policy supporters, this fruit came with lots of flies. Not only did North Korea dismiss the series of South Korean signals and cooperative gestures, it maintained and even stepped up its military provocations. These included a series of armed infiltration attempts (June 1998 submarine incident, July 1998 dead North Korean agent discovery, November 1998 submarine intrusion, December 1998 sinking of North Korean spy vessel, June 1999 North-South naval clash, etc.). It also included the August 1998 attempted launch of a long-range ballistic missile (allegedly a North Korean satellite) and construction in late 1998– early 1999 of additional launch facilities. The discovery of a large underground construction in the summer of 1998 that suggested a

---

[1]The Mt. Kumgang tour was a product of Chung Ju-yung's agreement with Kim Jong Il to pay the North Koreans nearly $1 billion over the following six years in exchange for the rights to develop this and several other projects. For details on this project and its role in the public debate, see Chapter Three.

continuing North Korean nuclear program in contravention of the 1994 U.S.-DPRK "Agreed Framework" completed the package. North Korea paired these provocative actions with increasingly belligerent rhetoric.

Not surprisingly, this behavior provoked anger among South Korean conservatives and sharp criticism of the government's approach toward North Korea. The intense U.S. focus on North Korea's nuclear and missile activities during this period indirectly reinforced this criticism, by strengthening South Korean skeptics who questioned the wisdom and efficacy of the sunshine policy. President Kim responded by reiterating the need to maintain deterrence and pursue dialogue simultaneously. He also increased his declaratory emphasis on national security and used the South Korean sinking of a North Korean spy ship in December 1998 to demonstrate his determination not to tolerate military provocations. This bolstered his position at home and helped dampen public debate.

At the same time, President Kim made clear he would continue to pursue engagement with North Korea. Giving early substance to this intention, he authorized the Hyundai group to proceed with the Mt. Kumgang tourist project in July 1998, despite the absence of a North Korean apology for the submarine incursion one month earlier.[2] Six months later—and less than one month after South Korea had sunk the North Korean spy vessel—he scaled back the administration's prior insistence on strict reciprocity in inter-Korean interactions to "flexible" reciprocity in a renewed attempt to establish government-to-government contacts. Insisting that there were signs of cautious change in the North, President Kim emphasized that he would continue to seek active engagement if Pyongyang showed a positive attitude.[3]

Administration leaders also moved to counter the growing disquiet in the United States over North Korean actions, which they understood could seriously jeopardize their sunshine policy. In intensive consultations with U.S. officials, they pressed the United States hard to seek a resolution of the nuclear and missile issues through diplo-

---

[2]*The Korea Times*, July 23, 1998.

[3]See the text of the president's "New Year's Message to the Nation," *The Korea Herald*, January 1, 1999.

matic engagement, a posture subsequently adopted in the U.S. policy review conducted by William Perry. They also pursued the idea of a comprehensive deal between Washington and Pyongyang involving resolution of the nuclear and missile issues in exchange for U.S. diplomatic recognition of the North and the lifting of economic sanctions.[4] One product of these intense discussions was the establishment of the Trilateral Coordination and Oversight Group (TCOG) to coordinate policies among the United States, Japan, and South Korea.

These dual sets of efforts to dampen domestic debate were aided by several other developments. One was the nationwide economic crisis, which focused almost everyone's attention on the implications of economic restructuring for his or her immediate situation.[5] Another was continued North Korean hostility. The absence of much actually happening in inter-Korean relations gave the debate about the administration's assumptions a somewhat theoretical quality. A third was the disarray in the GNP. This was caused partly by the difficulty it had adjusting to its new position as an opposition party and partly by its need to defend itself against allegations of involvement in a number of major scandals.[6] President Kim's coalition with Kim Jong-pil probably also played a role. While the ULD leader criticized the sunshine policy and worked to derail it from within, he also publicly emphasized the importance of avoiding war, even at the cost of delaying unification, and suggested that the public could have confidence in the government because he was in it. Such statements undoubtedly helped alleviate concerns among South Korean conservatives about the intent and direction of the sunshine policy.

---

[4] *The Korea Herald*, December 8, 1998.

[5] As one measure of this focus, the number of articles published by the conservative *Chosun Ilbo* and the progressive *Hankyoreh Sinmun* in 1998 and 1999 on economic reform and restructuring was more than ten times the number each paper published on the sunshine policy during the same period. For a flavor of the times, see Doh-jong Kim, "The Sunshine Policy and Domestic Political Dynamics: Political Implications for South Korea's Engagement Policy Toward North Korea," *National Strategy* (*Kukga Junryak*), Vol. 6, No. 1 (Seoul: Sejong Institute, 2000).

[6] The party and its leader were accused of having colluded with North Korea to help determine the outcome of different elections in South Korea and having diverted tax revenues for use in the party's presidential election campaign. All these accusations proved unfounded except for the last one, which is still being adjudicated.

In response, the general public's support for the sunshine policy remained high throughout this period. Preoccupied with the economic crisis and seeing little change in North Korea, most citizens were happy to have the focus shift away from unification—with its huge attendant costs—toward long-term peaceful coexistence. While they had little confidence that the government's new policy would produce significant changes in North Korea, they sensed that the threat from the North was declining and welcomed a more protracted approach to unification.[7] Accordingly, the public debate was relatively restrained throughout this period. Although public criticism always existed, and was strong in certain quarters, it was not strong enough to precipitate a major national debate or significantly affect the direction of government policy.

SUMMER (JANUARY 2000 TO JUNE 2000)

Despite the relatively restrained debate, the president faced substantial obstacles to moving forward with his policy agenda, not only in the National Assembly but also within his own governing coalition. With the South Korean economy beginning to show signs of recovery from the financial crisis by the beginning of 2000 and his sunshine policy at a standstill, he looked for ways to change the underlying conditions. What he came up with was a new political party. Although not widely appreciated outside of Korean political circles, the president's decision to found the MDP marked a significant turning point both in the public debate over the sunshine policy and in South Korean politics.

The decision reflected the president's determination to overcome his domestic political difficulties—caused in large part by his party's minority position within the National Assembly—as a means for pursuing his larger policy objectives. At the top of these objectives was engineering a historic breakthrough in ties with North Korea. The president made the linkage between the establishment of a new

---

[7]Norman D. Levin, *The Shape of Korea's Future: South Korean Attitudes Toward Unification and Long-Term Security Issues* (Santa Monica, Calif.: RAND, 1999). This report analyzes the findings from a February 1999 public opinion poll conducted jointly by RAND and the *JoongAng Ilbo*. The survey focused on South Korean attitudes toward unification and long-term security issues.

party and his North Korea policy ambitions explicit himself. On the day the MDP was inaugurated (January 19, 2000), he communicated his plan to seek a North-South summit if his new party did well in the upcoming (April 13, 2000) parliamentary elections.[8]

From this point on, the name of the game changed. Instead of pursuing his sunshine policy goals by seeking a broad national consensus based on his coalition with the conservative ULD, President Kim sought to expand his own independent power base so as to give him greater latitude in making policy. His calculation was clear: Increased latitude would increase the likelihood of policy success; policy success would not only advance his goals vis-a-vis North Korea but further strengthen his domestic political position. A successful summit with the North, he clearly was wagering, was essential to both.

Having made this decision and founded the MDP, Kim worked hard to induce members of the other parties to defect and join his new party. He also encouraged progressive NGOs to support the MDP and cooperate with the government in seeking to change South Korea's politics and culture more broadly. As a down payment, the president endorsed the campaign by a large coalition of civic groups and NGOs to blacklist "corrupt" or "unfit" politicians. The goal was to either deny them party endorsements or, if endorsed, prevent their victory in the April parliamentary elections. All this, to no one's surprise, outraged the GNP and ULD since they were the primary targets (as well as chief victims) of the president's actions. In the process, it became a major source of friction and distrust between the ruling and opposition parties.

At the same time, President Kim moved on his second track of seeking a North-South summit. Internally, he switched his right-hand man, Lim Dong-Won, from Minister of Unification to director of the National Intelligence Service, where Lim had more opportunity to pursue secret contacts with North Korea. Externally, he looked for a site where he could send a major public signal to the North without provoking heated political reactions in South Korea. The site chosen, replete with symbolism, was Berlin, the capital of a unified Germany.

---

[8]*The Korea Herald*, January 21, 2000. President Kim formally proposed this summit one week later (January 26) in his annual New Year's press conference.

On March 9, President Kim gave a speech there on the last leg of an extended European visit outlining a new set of proposals to North Korea for ending the Cold War structure on the Korean Peninsula.[9] Subsequently labeled the "Berlin Declaration," the speech made four points explicit:

- The South Korean government would support North Korea's economic recovery—for which the two governments should assume responsibility given constraints on the private sector—and would actively promote large-scale economic collaboration in a broad range of industrial, infrastructure, and other areas.

- It would participate in joint efforts to end the Cold War on the peninsula and create a system for peaceful coexistence.

- It strongly wanted to arrange reunions of families separated by the Korean War.

- It wanted to reopen political dialogue and exchange official envoys between the two sides to explore how to move forward in these areas and resolve outstanding problems.

Perhaps as salient to North Korean leaders as any of these four explicit points was what was missing from the Berlin Declaration: any suggestion that South Korea would link its economic assistance to concessions by North Korea on military threat and tension reduction measures.

Following the speech, secret contacts between the two Koreas to arrange a summit meeting intensified. As a result of these contacts, and expressed North Korean willingness to exchange special envoys to discuss such a summit, President Kim appointed Park Jie-won, then Minister of Culture and Tourism, to be his representative. After four secret meetings between March 17 and April 8, the two special envoys reached agreement.[10] On April 10, three days before South Korea's national parliamentary elections, both sides announced they had agreed to hold an inter-Korean summit.

---

[9]"Address by President Kim Dae Jung at the Free University of Berlin, March 9, 2000," *Korea and World Affairs*, Vol. 24, No. 1, Spring 2000, pp. 131–137.

[10]Ministry of Unification, *Peace and Cooperation—White Paper on Korean Unification 2001* (Seoul: Ministry of Unification, 2001), pp. 31–32.

President Kim's bet that success with his sunshine policy would yield domestic political dividends paid off almost immediately, at least somewhat. Although the MDP did not succeed in becoming the majority party in the National Assembly elections three days later, it did increase its seats from 79 in the previous elections to 115, as shown in Table 1, narrowing its gap with the GNP to only 18 seats. It also won seats in districts virtually throughout the country (the main exception being the conservative stronghold of the southeast Yong-nam region), effectively establishing itself as a national party rather than simply as a party based only in a single region (the southwest-ern Cholla provinces).[11] As a result of the election, the MDP ex-panded its share of total National Assembly seats from 26.4 percent in the preceding election to 42.1 percent, a significant increase.

To be sure, the MDP triumph was qualified: The GNP still out-polled it 39 percent to 35.9 percent. Moreover, the GNP actually *increased* its share of National Assembly seats from 46.5 percent to 48.7 percent of the total. Only four seats short of a majority, it remained the na-tion's largest political party. By receiving just 3.1 percent less of the total national vote than did the GNP, however, the MDP established itself convincingly as the only major contender to the GNP-led con-servatives in an increasingly two-party dominant system. This was reinforced by the showing of the other parties. Kim Jong-pil's ULD garnered only 9.8 percent of the total popular vote, a whopping 10 percent less than it had received in the previous election. It fell from 50 seats to 17, losing its status as a negotiating body in the National Assembly. Splinter parties did even more poorly.

Table 1

Distribution of National Assembly Seats by Political Party

	NCNP(1996)/ MDP(2000)	NKP(1996)/ GNP(2000)	ULD	Other Parties
April 1996	79	139	50	16
April 2000	115	133	17	8

[11] Doh-jong Kim and Hyung-joon Kim, "Analysis of the 16th National Assembly Elec-tion," *Korea Focus*, Vol. 8, No. 3, May–June 2000, p. 2.

Along with this short-term benefit, however, came some longer-term costs. The biggest came from the announcement of the summit meeting only three days before the elections. It is hard to exaggerate the importance of this event. First, it infuriated the opposition parties, who saw it as an egregious attempt to influence the outcome of the elections and manipulate a nonpartisan issue—the universal Korean desire for reunification—for domestic political purposes.[12] Second, it spawned a range of conspiracy and corruption allegations that fostered public cynicism and undermined support for the government's policy.[13] Third, it reignited questions about the administration's trustworthiness and credibility by demonstrating that the government had been dealing with the North Koreans behind the scenes, despite its repeated pledges to make its approach to the North completely open and transparent. Added to this are the intense personal feelings in South Korea toward Kim Dae Jung himself. For those who congenitally hate the president, the announcement that he would be the one going to Pyongyang was simply anathema. While none of these groups could challenge the idea of a North-South summit itself, they were outraged by the administration's handling of the whole matter and determined to seek retribution.

The summit, held two months later in Pyongyang, was the sunshine policy's crowning moment. As the first meeting ever between the leaders of the two Koreas, and with its demonstrable, if still implicit, recognition of the ROK by the Communist North, the fact of the meeting itself made the summit a truly historic event. The Joint Declaration announced at the end of the summit reinforced the sense of a momentous breakthrough toward inter-Korean reconciliation, by identifying a range of areas for cooperative efforts and committing Kim Jong Il to pay a return visit to Seoul. The warmth of

---

[12]*Hankyoreh Sinmun*, April 10, 2000.

[13]While one could always hear strong, even scurrilous, comments about Kim Dae Jung, the way the summit was announced took these to a new level. One allegation, for example, had to do with the amount of money the government had to pay Pyongyang to secure its agreement to the summit. According to those who believe this allegation, the reason why the summit was delayed one day at the last minute was because the money that was supposed to be handed over to the North in exchange for Kim Jong Il's agreement to have the summit had not yet been transferred. The administration allegedly then assessed South Korean companies the extra money required to enable the summit to go forward. Such allegations have recently been revived and have become a major issue in domestic South Korean politics.

Kim Jong Il's welcome to the southern delegates, moreover, visually reinforced this impression. Watching his performance on their television screens, many South Koreans wondered if everything they had been taught to believe about the man was sheer fiction.

No one was more swept away by the event though than President Kim. Returning to Seoul, he sounded more like a proselyte than president of the nation. "A new age has dawned for our nation," he said. "We have reached a turning point so that we can put an end to the history of territorial division." He then went on:

> I found that Pyongyang, too, was our land. The Pyongyang people are the same as us, the same nation sharing the same blood. Regardless of what they have been saying and [how they have been] acting outwardly, they have deep love and a longing for their compatriots in the South. If you talk with them, you notice that right away . . . . We must consider North Koreans as our brothers and sisters. We must believe that they have the same thought . . . . Most importantly there is no longer going to be any war. The North will no longer attempt unification by force and at the same time we will not do any harm to the North.[14]

Unfortunately for the president, not all South Koreans shared this halcyon vision. Indeed, for many, both the substance and process of the summit raised profound concerns. The struggle between these two perspectives raised the public debate to an entirely new level and heralded the onset of a new season.

FALL (JUNE 2000 TO JANUARY 2001)

The South Korean political environment heated up almost immediately. Images of the televised summit and President Kim's remarks upon returning to Seoul lit a fire under those with a "one-people" orientation and stimulated a wave of nationalism and unification euphoria throughout the country. The government encouraged this process by calling into question the validity of the image of Kim Jong Il traditionally fostered by South Korea's elite. This in turn stimu-

---

[14]Excerpted from the text of "President Kim Dae Jung's Remarks on Returning to Seoul from the Inter-Korean Summit in Pyongyang," as appeared in *The Korea Herald*, June 16, 2000.

lated broader debate about the legitimacy of the country's anti-Communism education. Progressive groups seized this momentum to try and undermine the position of conservatives in South Korean society more broadly, labeling them "pro–Cold War," "anti-unification," and "anachronistic."[15] Some branded anyone who raised questions about Kim Jong Il or suggested that the summit had certain shortcomings as a "foreigner" (i.e., not "true" Korean), a particularly inflammatory charge given Korea's history.

For his part, President Kim touted the success of his sunshine policy and mobilized progressive groups to rally behind the government. He emphasized three points in particular. First, he emphasized that the summit talks ended the danger of war on the peninsula or any North Korean attempt to achieve unification by force. Second, he emphasized that North Korea agreed to replace the provision in the Communist Party's platform calling for the liberation of the entire peninsula under socialism in return for corresponding steps by South Korea to replace its National Security Law. Third, he emphasized that Kim Jong Il agreed to a continued stationing of U.S. military forces in South Korea, even after reunification.

All of these points were aimed at strengthening President Kim's supporters and countering critics of the sunshine policy. All were also, however, highly contentious. Members of the military and others sensitive to national security concerns challenged the first point, noting the absence of any mention of the words "peace" and "security" in the summit's Joint Declaration and North Korea's refusal to discuss ways for reducing the military confrontation.[16] Conservative and even many moderate South Koreans dismissed the second point as designed by Pyongyang to stimulate instability in South Korea, rather than to renounce the North's historic goal of bringing the entire peninsula under its control. The mainstream press all questioned the third point, initially on the grounds that Kim Jong Il's alleged comment was made privately to President Kim and

---

[15]*Hankyoreh Sinmun*, June 16, 2000.

[16]Yong-Sup Han, "Did North Korea's Threat of War Really Disappear?" *JoongAng Ilbo*, June 20, 2000.

could not be authenticated and subsequently because of contradictory statements by North Korea itself.[17]

On top of this, the summit's Joint Declaration itself was highly controversial. As described in Chapter Four, this was partly because the declaration appeared to reflect much more of the North's agenda than the South's—raising questions about whether the president had somehow been "deceived" into accommodating the North's position. It was also, however, because many saw in the declaration an administration willingness to entertain a degree of political integration with Pyongyang not sanctioned by either previous government policy or prior national consensus. Critics assailed the administration more broadly for having shifted the focus of the summit away from ways to implement the 1992 "Basic Agreement" and achieve peaceful coexistence—the ostensible goal of the summit as expressed originally by South Korean leaders—to how to foster unification. The president's decision to repatriate to Pyongyang all long-term North Korean prisoners in South Korean jails without a corresponding move by the North to return South Korean prisoners of war held in the North further heightened domestic controversy and reinforced conservative charges of an imbalance in North-South relations.

This was just the beginning. With their sharply divergent ideological orientations and political agendas, progressive and conservative groups geared up for enhanced confrontation. The KCRC and other progressive NGOs organized collective activities to expedite North-South exchange and prepare for Kim Jong Il's return visit to Seoul. The *Hankyoreh* and other government supporters called into question not just the intentions of government critics in pointing out problems with the summit but also their patriotism. Liberal scholars pushed the bounds of previously accepted discourse on a range of taboo topics.[18] For their part, anti-U.S. and anti-U.S. military base

---

[17]The most explicit, albeit much later, example was the joint Russia-DPRK statement issued after Kim Jong Il's somewhat bizarre trip to Moscow in the fall of 2001, in which the North Korean leader explicitly insisted on the withdrawal of U.S. troops.

[18]One, for example, later went so far as to suggest that Kim Jong Il should not be held responsible for the Korean War since he was a child when it happened. Anything that even hinted at exculpating North Korea from responsibility for the Korean War was previously one of South Korea's major taboos. For Hwang Tae Yun's controversial remarks, see the *Chosun Ilbo*, February 27, 2001.

groups took this as a cue to step up their own activities. Citing the changed conditions due to the summit's success, they intensified their questioning of the need for a U.S. military presence. Many joined in larger coalitions with the CCEJ, PSPD, and other progressive forces to seek the closure of U.S. training facilities and revision of the U.S.-ROK Status of Forces Agreement. They also sought U.S. compensation for the killing of South Korean civilians during the Korean War (e.g., at Nogun-ri), for environmental damage caused by activities at U.S. military bases, and for a long list of other alleged offenses.

Conservative groups responded in kind. The GNP attacked the government for its "one-sided" assistance to North Korea and having played into the hands of North Korea's Communist leaders. The *Chosun Ilbo*, *Donga Ilbo*, and *JoongAng Ilbo* questioned the speed with which the administration was moving to expand inter-Korean cooperation, as well as its appropriateness. Conservative NGOs mobilized to ensure that a number of preconditions—including a North Korean apology for starting the Korean War and for conducting a slew of terrorist acts thereafter—be met before Kim Jong Il is allowed to visit Seoul.[19] Many conservatives attacked President Kim for being soft on defense and neglecting, if not endangering, South Korean security. Some denounced him and his Blue House staff as being "pro–North Korean" and "anti–liberal democracy."[20]

Two developments in the fall of 2000 heightened this confrontation further. One was the Nobel Committee's decision in October to award that year's Nobel Peace Prize to President Kim. Kim's supporters understandably saw the award as validating the president's sunshine approach toward North Korea, with some interpreting the award as confirming their broader political and ideological convictions. His detractors, however, while delighted that a South Korean had been so honored, were appalled that the South Korean honoree was their long-time antagonist. Many were alarmed that the award might stimulate further moves in a direction they considered injurious to South Korea's interests, if not morally inexcusable given the

---

[19]Sung Won Park, "Conservatives Looking for Counter-Offensive," *Shindonga*, September 2000, pp. 76–94.

[20]*JoongAng Ilbo*, July 13, 2000.

North's despotic rule and human rights abuses. Thus, in a curious sort of way, the award energized groups on both ends of the political spectrum.

The other, more serious development was the response of North Korea after the summit. This took the form of a two-track approach. One involved intensified efforts by Pyongyang to split South Korean society. North Korea reduced its public criticism of the ROK government by roughly 75 percent in the months after the summit, for example. At the same time, it repeatedly urged South Koreans to uphold the June 15 Joint Declaration and branded South Korean "ultraconservatives" and "rightists" as being "anti-unification."[21] This track also involved a series of highly charged activities designed to stoke emotions, and divisions, in South Korea. These included, for example, allowing North Korean athletes to march alongside their South Korean counterparts behind a single flag at the opening ceremony of the Sydney Olympics and inviting leftist South Korean workers to visit North Korea for "debates" with their North Korean counterparts on unification.[22]

The other track involved efforts to bypass South Korea entirely and deal with the United States instead. North Korea sent National Defense Committee Vice Chairman Cho Myong Rok to Washington, hosted a visit by U.S. Secretary of State Albright to Pyongyang, and invited U.S. President Clinton to Pyongyang—all in an effort to utilize North Korea's missile program as a vehicle for normalizing U.S.-DPRK relations. At the same time, it dragged out a series of inter-Korean talks, apparently buying time to see what would come out of its talks with the United States. Except for two emotion-laden reunions of 100 families separated by the Korean War, it implemented none of

---

[21]The North's definition of these latter folks included the GNP's Lee Hoi Chang, former President Kim Young Sam, and pretty much anyone who expressed reservations about the summit or criticisms of the sunshine policy.

[22]Later in 2001 North and South Korean labor unions drafted a joint manifesto calling for an inter-Korean labor forum for unification. The draft advocated a formula for unification—"one people, one nation, two systems, two independent governments"—that was basically the same as North Korea's position. Such transparent efforts to exacerbate social tensions in South Korea by manipulating South Korean civic organizations violated North Korea's pledge at the summit to address inter-Korean issues directly through government-to-government talks. They also significantly inflamed debate in South Korea. *JoongAng Ilbo*, July 26, 2001.

North added to the difficulties. These further impeded North-South economic interactions and exacerbated the administration's difficulty in demonstrating the fruits of its sunshine activities. Indirectly, they contributed to a more intrinsic administration tendency to oversell the results of its policies and reinforced the growing public confusion.

Along with this increased confusion came increased polarization. The political spectrum of South Korean society increasingly divided into what many on the left described as "pro-unification" and "anti-unification" camps.[27] The government appeared to see the situation in equally stark terms, officially characterizing the public as divided between "the Cold War era psychology and a new mindset of the post–Cold War world."[28] This trend toward sharp ideological polarization was bolstered by the tendency of both sides to search for evidence in postsummit developments for their respective policy positions. As attitudes hardened with the approach of "winter," this evidence was not hard to find.

WINTER (JANUARY 2001 TO OCTOBER 2002)

President Bush's victory in the U.S. presidential election became the last benchmark in the debate's evolution to date. South Koreans had long speculated on how a Republican Party victory might affect U.S. policies toward Korea, particularly the Kim Dae Jung government's approach toward North Korea. They knew that an important part of the party's base has a visceral distaste for North Korea, considers the Clinton administration's approach to have constituted "appeasement," and strongly favors a tougher approach to alleged North Korean "blackmail." As a general statement, those on the South Korean left approached the prospect of a Republican administration with concern and those on the right approached it with varying degrees of anticipation.

---

[27]Jang-Hee Lee, "Domestic Tasks Left Behind the South-North Summit Meeting," an unpublished paper prepared for a Sejong Institute conference on May 11, 2001.

[28]Ministry of Unification, *Four Years of Policy Toward North Korea*, February 26, 2002. A copy is available online at the ministry's web site, www.unikorea.go.kr.

North Korea preempted both sides, putting substantive progress in inter-Korean talks on hold pending changes in South Korea and clarification of Bush's "hard-line" position.[29] It is possible that the North was alarmed by the prospect of potential policy changes in Washington and wanted to signal the new U.S. president not to alter direction. This interpretation is supported by North Korea's insistence that it would not engage in talks with the new administration unless these talks began with the same positions taken by the Clinton administration before it left office. It is also possible, however, that Pyongyang simply saw an opportunity to drive a wedge between Washington and Seoul, while increasing its bargaining leverage over the United States and inflaming South Korean opinion. Either way, the unspoken message was the same: Reconciliation with the ROK is subordinate to U.S.-DPRK relations.

Concerned about North Korean foot-dragging and anxious to enlist the new U.S. administration in support of South Korea's sunshine approach, President Kim pushed hard for an early U.S.-ROK summit. Not nearly ready for such a summit but also not anxious to turn down a valued ally, President Bush agreed. The summit, held in Washington on March 7, 2001, must rank among the more curious in U.S.-ROK diplomatic history. Rarely has there been less correlation between cause and effect.

Here is what officially happened:[30]

---

[29]The North agreed in inter-Korean talks in early February on a series of cooperative steps to facilitate the removal of land mines from the demilitarized zone so as to allow the reconnection of the Seoul-Sinuiju railway line, as agreed upon the previous summer. It declared it would not implement the agreement, however, until South Korea stopped referring to the North as its "main enemy." It simultaneously stepped up its anti-U.S. rhetoric, threatening to end its moratorium on missile tests and abandon the Agreed Framework in view of the Bush administration's new "hard-line" attitude. This was within a month of President Bush's inauguration and before he had even assembled many top members of his administration. See Donald G. Gross, "Slow Start in U.S. Policy toward the DPRK," *Comparative Connections*, April 2001, pp. 34–35. The online text is available at www.csis.org/pacfor/cc/0101Qus_skorea.html.

[30]*Joint Statement Between the United States of America and the Republic of Korea,* March 7, 2001. The text is available at www.whitehouse.gov/news/releases/2001/03/20010307-2.html.

- The two presidents publicly agreed that reconciliation and cooperation between the two Koreas contribute not only to peace on the Korean Peninsula but to stability throughout the region.

- President Bush expressed support for the ROK government's policy of engagement with North Korea.

- He endorsed President Kim's leading role in resolving inter-Korean issues.

- He also shared the South Korean leader's hope that a second inter-Korean summit would make a further contribution to inter-Korean relations and regional security.

- Both presidents also reaffirmed their commitment to the 1994 Agreed Framework and called on North Korea to join in taking steps to ensure its successful implementation.

- The two leaders then discussed their respective worldviews, concurring that the global security environment is fundamentally different than during the Cold War and requires new approaches to deterrence and defense.

- They ended their official meeting by agreeing on the importance of close consultations and coordination on policy toward North Korea and the need to work together to support South Korea's economic reform efforts and address bilateral trade issues.

Even if this had not come from a Republican president, this would appear to have been a substantial achievement from South Korea's perspective. The fact that President Kim was the first Asian leader invited to the White House, reflecting an intentional effort by the Bush administration to communicate the importance it places on U.S.-ROK relations, might appear to have reinforced this impression.

So much for appearances. As it happens, in off-hand comments to the press after the official meeting, President Bush alluded candidly to his deep distrust of Kim Jong Il and emphasized the need for "reciprocity" and "adequate verification" of any missile agreement that might be reached with North Korea. He also expressed his personal doubts over whether this would be possible in the North Korean case given the extremely closed nature of the system. Noting that his administration was in the midst of the policy review he had promised during his election campaign, he indicated that the United

States would not seek to resume missile talks with North Korea until this review was finished.

The impact of these comments was almost instantaneous. North Korea denounced the United States for trying to prevent inter-Korean reconciliation and indefinitely postponed the next scheduled round of inter-Korean ministerial talks (as if *indefinitely postponing* North-South dialogue would *hasten* inter-Korean reconciliation). South Korea back-pedaled by giving new rhetorical emphasis to precisely those issues—how to reactivate the 1992 Basic Agreement, reduce military tensions, and establish a peace process on the peninsula—that had been omitted from the June 2000 inter-Korean summit agenda.[31] And everyone in South Korea blamed everyone else for what all agreed was a major diplomatic failure. Over the next several months, public debate intensified sharply in South Korea, with U.S. policy becoming a central, hot button issue.

It is hard to exaggerate the role of the South Korean media in creating this situation. Although many agreements had been reached between Seoul and Pyongyang, and many more were constantly being predicted, little of substance actually happened in North-South relations in the seven months between the June 2000 summit and the January 2001 inauguration of President Bush. Despite this, the South Korean media explicitly and intentionally linked the "stalemate" between the two Koreas with the policies of the new U.S. administration. The universality of this response might appear somewhat strange given the wide political and ideological differences among the media. In fact, it reflects a broadly shared interest.

On the conservative right, the *Chosun Ilbo*, *Donga Ilbo*, and other media saw President Bush's personal reservations about North Korea as confirmation of their own position. As recently as one month be-

---

[31]See, for example, President Kim's speech to a joint American Enterprise Institute/Council on Foreign Relations luncheon the day after his meeting with President Bush, described in *The Korea Times*, March 9, 2001. President Kim reinforced this emphasis shortly after returning to Seoul, appointing Lim Dong-Won as the Minister of Unification to rejigger the presentation, at least, of South Korea's policy. Ambassador Lim did precisely this. His inaugural speech as Minister of Unification stressed three themes: cooperation without peace has obvious limits, visible measures for building military confidence and easing tension need to be implemented between the two Koreas, and policy needs to be predicated on both domestic support and cooperation with the United States. Excerpts from his talk are in *The Korea Times*, March 28, 2001.

fore Bush's inauguration they had been forced to watch President Kim bask in world acclaim as he received the Nobel Peace Prize. They fairly jumped at this modest sign of external validation. Encouraged that South Korea's major ally shared their own doubts, they suggested that President Bush's "skepticism" was directed not only at Kim Jong Il but also at President Kim himself and warned of a split between South Korea and its chief ally over how to deal with North Korea.

For their part, the *Hankyoreh Sinmun* and other media groups on the left interpreted President Bush's comments as confirming *their* own views: The United States is driven by its hegemonic goal of dominating the world and sees Korean unification as a threat to its strategic interests. They saw in President Bush's comments the means for mobilizing South Korean progressives to advance their "one-people" unification objectives, while heightening anti-American feeling and opposition to the U.S. military presence in South Korea. They also found in U.S. policy a rationale for North Korean inaction. Not surprisingly, they seized on these comments to stimulate nationalist sentiment and portray the United States as an obstacle to North-South reconciliation.

What had actually happened at the March summit meeting, of course, was that the U.S. publicly endorsed South Korea's engagement policy—a message President Bush strongly reinforced two months later in a letter to President Kim—while it implied that its own approach would be more cautious. This general orientation became official policy when the United States announced the result of its policy review in June. The official statement by President Bush made three points explicit:[32]

- The United States would "undertake serious discussions with North Korea on a broad agenda." This would include "improved implementation of the Agreed Framework," "verifiable constraints" on North Korea's missile programs and ban on its missile exports, and a "less threatening conventional military posture."

---

[32]The text is available at www.whitehouse.gov/news/releases/2001/06/20010611-4.html.

- It would pursue these discussions as part of a "comprehensive approach" to the North that seeks to "encourage progress toward North-South reconciliation, peace on the Korean Peninsula, a constructive relationship with the United States, and greater stability in the region."

- And the United States would be willing to ease sanctions, expand assistance, and "take other political steps" if North Korea "responds affirmatively and takes appropriate action."

Secretary of State Powell underlined these points the following day.[33] In a briefing for the press after his talks with the South Korean foreign minister, Powell emphasized three things in particular: The United States is "prepared to resume an enhanced dialogue with North Korea on issues of mutual interest to both nations." It is "not setting any preconditions" for this dialogue but hopes it will be "an open dialogue on all of the issues that are of concern." In addition, it is prepared in the meantime to maintain the Agreed Framework. Stressing the administration's desire to move forward "in a more comprehensive way" to address the range of issues bedeviling North Korea's relations with the United States, he expressed the "hope" that the long-pending return visit by Kim Jong Il to Seoul "can now be put back on track." Secretary Powell reinforced these points during his visit to Seoul in late July, publicly stressing the "without pre-conditions" aspect of the U.S. proposal and urging Russian President Putin to persuade Pyonyang to resume negotiations with the United States.

The announcement of the U.S. policy review results was critical. Although the United States had made it unmistakably clear that it was prepared to resume a "serious" and "unconditional" dialogue, North Korea refused to take "yes" for an answer. Instead, it accused the United States of attempting to put "conditions" on the resumption of talks and rebuffed the offer. Kim Jong Il also stiffed repeated pleas by President Kim to pay a return visit to Seoul and resume the North-South dialogue. Instead, he turned his attention to improving North Korea's ties with Russia and China, taking a long, meandering train trip across Siberia to Moscow in late July and early August and host-

---

[33]The transcript was distributed by the Office of International Information Programs, U.S. Department of State, and is available through http://usinfo.state.gov.

ing a visit by Chinese President Jiang Zemin to Pyongyang in the beginning of September. All this turned South Korean public opinion decidedly against North Korea and weakened support for the government's sunshine policy.

The state of the South Korean economy contributed to the mounting domestic tensions. After showing signs of recovery from the financial crisis at the beginning of 2000 (growth increased by 10.7 percent in 1999), the economy slowed significantly in 2001 in part because of the larger global slowdown. Growth rates projected in the 6–7 percent range at the beginning of the year were more than halved as both exports and imports dropped sharply and corporate investment faltered.[34] Economic anxieties further weakened diminishing South Korean willingness to provide assistance to North Korea. Among other things, the economy exacerbated the government's difficulties in trying to prop up Hyundai's floundering Mt. Kumgang project. It also hindered the government's ability to use aid as a lubricant for broader North-South interactions.

In response, the progressive media and NGOs stepped up their efforts to defend the sunshine policy, shifting blame for the stalemate in inter-Korean relations almost entirely to the United States. To make this argument they broadened the bill of particulars. According to them, the United States was exaggerating the threat from North Korea not only to force the ROK to buy advanced U.S. weapons and ensure a continued troop presence in South Korea but also to provide an excuse for developing missile defenses that would ensure U.S. global hegemony. This effort would prevent North-South reconciliation, while provoking a major arms race and ushering in a new Cold War in Asia. One of the networks created by these groups, the Committee for Collective Measures to Prevent Missile Defense and Realize Peace, generated within a couple days a letter signed by more than 100 civic group representatives demanding an end to missile defense and America's "Cold War" mentality.

The GNP, conservative media, and other groups on the right launched a counteroffensive. They denounced their leftist opponents as dangerous, destructive forces, tearing South Korean society

---

[34]Korea Economic Institute, *Korea Insight,* Vol. 4, No. 2, February 2002.

apart in the name of "one people" and maliciously fostering anti-American sentiment among the public.[35] They also attacked the government for a wide range of alleged offenses. They criticized the government for its lax handling of North Korea's repeated encroachments of South Korean territorial waters in June, for example, denouncing in particular its alleged "political intervention" to prevent a tough military response that might further set back North-South relations.[36] They challenged the administration's effort to divert government funds to aid Hyundai, which was facing bankruptcy from losses stemming from the Mt. Kumgang project. They also assailed the government repeatedly for its "one-way" assistance policy, citing the Bush administration's emphasis on reciprocity and verification as the only way to deal with North Korea.

In this environment, three developments significantly weakened the government and raised the volume of debate to yet a new level. One was the visit by Kim Jong Il to Moscow in late July and early August. At the end of his talks with Russian President Putin, the two sides issued a joint communiqué that publicly alluded to North Korea's insistence on the withdrawal of U.S. troops from Korea. Normally such boilerplate rhetoric from North Korea would not receive much attention. But in the heated environment existing at the time, opponents of the sunshine policy rushed to point out the contradiction between this official document and Kim Dae Jung's assertion that Kim Jong Il had expressed his acceptance of a continued U.S. military presence in South Korea. Gaining this acceptance in his private conversations with the North Korean leader, President Kim had long insisted, was one of his major accomplishments at the June 2000 summit. The clear contradiction between these two statements undermined the president's credibility and political standing in South Korea.

The second development was the government's decision to prosecute the leading conservative newspaper companies for alleged tax evasion and other financial wrongdoing. Technically, this decision was much broader than just the conservative papers. The government brought civil charges against 23 major media institutions, in-

---

[35]*Chosun Ilbo*, June 8, 2001.

[36]*Chosun Ilbo*, June 6, 2001.

cluding virtually every national news organization, and assessed them fines of nearly $400 million for having evaded taxes.[37] It also fined 16 individuals within these companies roughly $23 million for irregular business transactions. But the clear target was the major conservative press—the *Chosun Ilbo, Donga Ilbo, JoongAng Ilbo,* and *Kookmin Ilbo*—which was fined the overwhelming bulk of the $400 million in back taxes and penalties. The magnitude of the fines was without precedent.[38] The government followed up in August by arresting the owners of the *Chosun Ilbo, Donga Ilbo,* and *Kookmin Ilbo* on charges of embezzlement and tax evasion.

Predictably, the left and right were sharply split in their reactions. Progressive groups—in what appears to most Westerners as a clear case of ideology trumping principle—supported the government's attack. They denounced the "shamelessness" of the "corrupt family-owned press" and demanded major "reform" of the (conservative) media. Conservatives, on the other hand, strongly criticized the government, while the major newspapers waged a life and death struggle in the name of "freedom of the press."[39] Although the public generally agreed that financial wrongdoings should not be permitted, it almost universally saw the government's escalating war on the press as a transparent attempt to silence its critics—particularly those opposing the sunshine policy. The general presumption was that, in trying to stifle or at least intimidate these papers, the government was seeking to improve both the prospects for a return visit by Kim Jong Il to Seoul and the ruling party's prospects in the upcoming presidential election.[40]

At the height of this war between the government and the conservative media, foreign press organizations and public figures began to

---

[37] *The New York Times,* July 3, 2001.

[38] David Steinberg, "The Korean Press and Orthodoxy," *Chosun Daily* (English edition), July 17, 2001.

[39] Even the ULD, although still in the ruling coalition at this point, opposed the government's attack on the media and publicly asked the ruling camp not to arrest the owners of the major newspaper companies. *The Korea Times*, August 20, 2001.

[40] A political reporter for the *Hankyoreh Sinmun* suggested in a book published that year that the effort to destroy the big three newspapers was preplanned by the Blue House. Han-yong Sung, *Why Did DJ Fail to Resolve the Regional Conflict?* (Seoul: Joongsim, 2001).

express concern over the South Korean government's actions.[41] The conservative Korea Bar Association adopted a resolution criticizing the government for having "regressed away from the real rule of law" and urging it to pursue its reform programs "based on the rule of law, not on [the] rule of power."[42] Also, members of the opposition parties began talking about the need to consider impeaching the president.[43] Rumors spread among conservatives that the MDP was planning to revise the constitution to enable President Kim to remain in power and promote his unification objectives.[44]

All this further inflamed the debate over the government's handling of policy toward North Korea and sharply constrained the government's latitude for action. It also fed the growing mood of scandal surrounding the Blue House, as the mainstream press went after government officials (including several government prosecutors and tax officials who were subsequently sent to prison for bribery) and close associates of the president for their own wrongdoing. Progressive leaders in particular emphasize the importance of these scandals in damaging the president's moral legitimacy among the public and weakening his political authority. Perhaps the biggest effect, though, was that it contributed to Kim Jong-pil's subsequent decision to bolt the ruling coalition. As a result of this decision, the government lost its majority in the National Assembly, the Blue House Secretary for Policy stepped down, and President Kim resigned his position as president of the ruling party.

The third development was North Korea's August 15 celebration of Korea's liberation from Japan. A group of more than 300 delegates from South Korea participated in this highly politicized event. While

---

[41]A letter by eight U.S. Congressmen to President Kim expressing concern over a possible infringement on press freedom received particularly big play. *JoongAng Ilbo*, English edition, July 19, 2001.

[42]*JoongAng Ilbo*, English edition, July 25, 2001.

[43]Hyung-jin Kim, op. cit.

[44]Reflecting the intensity of the distrust they feel for President Kim, if nothing else, many conservatives believe that the original plan was for Kim Jong Il to come to Seoul in the second half of 2000, whereupon both sides would issue a joint declaration of unification. On this basis, the administration would then change the ROK constitution to adopt a parliamentary system of government. This would obviate the need for presidential elections, hence terminating the "one-term" restriction against President Kim remaining in office.

there, some of the delegates attended festivities at a site honoring former North Korean leader Kim Il Sung's unification formula and engaged in other political activities praising the current leader, Kim Jong Il. By doing so, they knowingly violated both South Korea's National Security Law, which forbids these kinds of "pro–North Korea" activities, as well as an explicit pledge the delegation had made to the South Korean government not to do so in exchange for permission to attend the event.

News of this development hit South Korea like a bombshell. The conservative press viciously attacked the government's handling of the incident and called for a review of its engagement policy toward Pyongyang. The opposition parties demanded the arrest of the perpetrators and the resignation of Minister of Unification Lim Dong-Won.[45] A confrontation occurred at Kimpo Airport when the delegates returned to Seoul, with members of the Korea Veterans Association and other conservative organizations on one side and leaders of the Korean Association of Students and other progressive groups on the other. Although Minister Lim apologized for the entire incident, he refused to resign.

North Korea then intervened in an apparent effort to rescue the architect of the administration's sunshine policy. Breaking a six-month refusal to engage in talks with South Korea or even respond to the administration's repeated entreaties, it proposed restarting inter-Korean ministerial meetings on the eve of a National Assembly no-confidence vote for Lim Dong-Won in early September. Kim Jong-pil, along with most other South Koreans, saw this as a transparent attempt by the North to influence the outcome of the assembly vote. Outraged, he joined with the opposition and the vote passed. Minister Lim resigned the next day, bringing down the entire cabinet in the process.

The administration put on a brave face and tried to move forward. It accepted the North's proposal for restarting talks and hosted the fifth inter-Korean ministerial talks in Seoul from September 15–18. These talks (originally scheduled for the previous March but canceled by Pyongyang on the day they were to start) produced a lengthy list of

---

[45] *The Korea Times*, August 22, 2001.

agreements for future meetings, including a sixth round of inter-Korean ministerial talks in October.[46] The administration initiated talks with the North in early October on revitalizing the Mt. Kumgang project. Also, a week later, it exchanged lists with Pyongyang of family members who would participate in the next round of family reunions, scheduled for mid-October. In addition, the government moved to simplify regulations on inter-Korean exchanges, while continuing to urge Kim Jong Il to honor his summit commitment to come to Seoul.

These efforts went nowhere, however, primarily because of North Korea's continuing antics. For example, North Korea unilaterally canceled the family reunions scheduled for mid-October four days before they were to take place, ostensibly over the enhanced security alert adopted by South Korea in the wake of the September 11 terrorist attacks on the United States. It suddenly insisted that the next round of inter-ministerial talks—which until then had rotated between the two capitals—could be held only at North Korea's Mt. Kumgang resort, which delayed the talks for nearly two weeks until South Korea capitulated on the venue. It also refused to allow progress in these talks once they were held in mid-November, ostensibly because of the "hard-line" stance taken by South Korea's new foreign minister. The ministerial talks thus ended without either a joint statement or any bilateral agreements. Such actions sent almost all South Koreans to the exits. Even North Korea's strongest Southern soul mates, like the *Hankyoreh Sinmun*, criticized its actions. No one, it seemed, could say anything positive about Pyongyang.

President Kim's lame duck status effectively dates to these developments. The long North Korean freeze on substantive dialogue and repeated provocative behavior had taken its toll, seriously weakening Kim Dae Jung politically, souring public attitudes toward the North, and undermining support for the government's policy. As the world increasingly turned its attention to the war on terrorism, much of the remaining air was sucked out of the sunshine policy. With this, winter settled hard over engagement with North Korea.

---

[46]For details, see Aidan Foster-Carter, op. cit., 2001, available at www.csis.org/pacfor/cc/0103Qnk_sk.html.

The bleak scene was reinforced by a series of U.S. actions and official policy statements. In mid-October President Bush warned North Korea not to try to exploit U.S. involvement in Afghanistan, and he backed up the warning by deploying additional fighter aircraft to South Korea to compensate for the deployment of a U.S. aircraft carrier from the North Pacific to South Asia. In late November, President Bush demanded that North Korea allow international inspections of its suspected weapons of mass destruction (WMD) activities and terminate its destabilizing sale of missiles and missile technology. Also, in mid-December President Bush formally withdrew from the 1972 Anti-Ballistic Missile treaty, warning of the danger from "rogue states"—a term widely used for years to describe countries like North Korea—"who seek weapons of mass destruction."[47] The 2002 Nuclear Posture Review (NPR) completed in early January 2002 and subsequently leaked to the press drove home how seriously the Pentagon viewed such states. The NPR called among other things for the development of new nuclear weapons, especially "earth-penetrating" weapons that could destroy underground bunkers and facilities, that would be better suited to hit targets in countries like North Korea. It also described a range of contingencies for which such weapons might be used, all of which explicitly applied to North Korea.[48]

The "axis of evil" remark in President Bush's January 29, 2002, State of the Union speech formally elevated Pyongyang to the pantheon of regimes deemed to pose a "grave and growing danger" to U.S. and

---

[47]"Remarks by the President on National Missile Defense," December 13, 2001. A copy is available on the White House web site at www.whitehouse.gov/news/releases/2001/12/print/20011213-4.html.

[48]In setting requirements for U.S. nuclear strike capabilities, the NPR explicitly identified North Korea as one among a handful of states that "could be involved" in all three of the contingencies for which the United States must be prepared—"immediate, potential, or unexpected contingencies." "All have longstanding hostility toward the United States and its security partners," the review continued, and "North Korea and Iraq in particular have been chronic military concerns. All sponsor or harbor terrorists, and all have active WMD and missile programs." Department of Defense, *Nuclear Posture Review*, January 8, 2002, p. 16. For excerpts from the report from which this quotation is drawn, see www.globalsecurity.org/wmd/library/policy/dod/npr.htm.

global security.[49]   It was accompanied by other indications of U.S. concern. CIA Director George Tenet testified in Congress, for example, that North Korea was abiding by the Agreed Framework but only "that specific agreement with regard to that specific facility," implying that other disturbing activities were taking place elsewhere in the country.[50] This implication that North Korea might be involved in a hidden nuclear weapons program was reinforced on March 20 when President Bush, departing from his predecessor's routine practice, refused to certify that North Korea is abiding by the Agreed Framework's requirements. As one administration official put it, "This lays down a clear marker and puts the North Koreans on notice that we are gravely concerned."[51] It also communicated the sense of urgency growing in Washington during this period for North Korea to allow international inspectors access to facilities beyond the two nuclear reactors monitored under the Agreed Framework.

The "axis of evil" remark and related U.S. indications of concern unquestionably registered in North Korea. They also reverberated in South Korea, setting off a barrage of criticism in the National Assembly over President Kim's own policy and ratcheting up the existing recrimination between the ruling and opposition parties.[52] The speech had a polarizing impact more broadly.[53] Supporters of the sunshine policy predictably felt undercut and lashed out at the United States for "provoking war" and "undermining South Korean foreign policy." Opponents charged that the Kim administration's policies had created a "major gap" between Washington and Seoul, seriously weakening ROK security. In the wake of President Bush's speech, the South Korean foreign minister was summarily dismissed, student and radical NGO leaders organized intensive public demon-

---

[49]"The President's State of the Union Address," January 29, 2002. A copy is available on the White House web site at www.whitehouse.gov/news/releases/2002/01/print/20020129-11.html.

[50]Bates Gill, "A New Korean Nuclear Crisis?" *Newsweek Korea*, April 3, 2002.

[51]Peter Slevin, "N. Korea Not Following Nuclear Pact, U.S. to Say," *Washington Post*, March 20, 2002.

[52]Hong Kyudok, "South Korea-U.S. Cooperation on North Korea Policy," *Korea Focus*, Vol. 10, No. 2, March–April 2002.

[53]Donald G. Gross, "Riding the Roller-Coaster," *Comparative Connections*, 1st Quarter (January–March) 2002, available at www.csis.org/pacfor/cc/0201Qus_skorea.html.

strations, and official U.S.-ROK relations were thrown into turmoil. Many observers believe that it contributed to a perceptible rise in anti-American sentiment in South Korea.

For all their immediate and perhaps lingering effects in certain quarters, the "axis of evil" remark and related U.S. statements do not appear to have altered either the basic nature or course of the public debate over South Korean policies. Two subsequent developments contributed to attenuating their impact. One was President Bush's trip to Seoul in mid-February. In connection with this trip, the president reiterated the U.S. proposal for unconditional talks with North Korea. He expressed strong support for President Kim's engagement policy and publicly ruled out any U.S. military attack on North Korea, a statement even stronger than former President Clinton's assurance that the United States has "no hostile intent."[54] He also appealed to Chinese President Jiang Zemin on his way home from Seoul to impress on Pyongyang the U.S. desire for bilateral dialogue. Coming just a couple of weeks after his State of the Union address, the trip helped defuse rising emotions on both sides of the political and ideological divide in South Korea.

Secretary of State Powell helped lower temperatures further in February by publicly reemphasizing U.S. readiness to resume dialogue with Pyongyang "at any time the North Koreans decide to come back to the table."[55] In a major policy address a few months later, Powell reinforced this message by emphasizing U.S. readiness "to take important steps to help North Korea move its relations with the U.S. toward normalcy."[56] He also made clear that the United States, in return, wanted Pyongyang to "come into full compliance with the International Atomic Energy Agency safeguards that it agreed to when it signed the Nuclear Non-proliferation Treaty" and

---

[54]Ibid.:

> Bush's statement largely fulfilled North Korea's request that the new U.S. administration endorse former President Bill Clinton's North Korea policy before it would agree to resume bilateral talks with the United States.

[55]Secretary Colin L. Powell, "Statement on President Bush's Budget Request for FY 2003," before the House Appropriations Subcommittee on Foreign Operations, Export Financing, and Related Programs, February 13, 2002 [as prepared].

[56]Secretary Colin L. Powell, "Remarks at Asia Society Annual Dinner," New York, June 10, 2002, available at www.asiasociety.org/speeches/powell.htm.

address other issues on the U.S. agenda. While Powell's characterizations of North Korea remained unflattering, if not severe, his emphasis on U.S. willingness to engage with Pyongyang was reassuring to South Korean officials.

The second development involved the indications of an ongoing North Korean nuclear weapons program in violation of a series of solemn international commitments and related decision by South Korea to raise the priority of North Korean WMD activities on its own policy agenda. Such indications, to be sure, were not new. For several years U.S. intelligence analysts had suspected clandestine North Korean efforts—dating back apparently to the mid-1990s—to evade international controls on their development of nuclear weapons by switching from plutonium to uranium as the basis for their program. Circumstantial evidence developed into a pattern between 2000–2001 and, according to a report quoting high-ranking South Korean officials, was communicated to South Korea "by at least August 2001."[57] The United States and ROK are understood to have consulted closely thereafter.

Although U.S. leaders did not have a watertight case apparently until the summer of 2002, by the late winter and early spring of that year they had grown very concerned about North Korea's WMD programs. This was reflected in the U.S. policy statements described above. Concerned itself by the direction of events, South Korea raised the salience of the WMD issue in its own policies. Publicly warning of a potential crisis by 2003 that would rival the 1993–1994 crisis over North Korea's nuclear activities, the government decided to send Ambassador Lim as a special envoy to Pyongyang to transmit this concern directly to Kim Jong Il and try to restore North-South interactions.

The trip, from April 3–5, 2002, was at least partially successful. It enabled South Korea to convey to Pyongyang both the depth of U.S. concern and seriousness of its willingness to engage in dialogue. It narrowed the gap between U.S. and ROK approaches and capped rising tensions in U.S.-ROK relations. It helped dampen public anxi-

---

[57]For further details, see Doug Struck and Glenn Kessler, "Hints on N. Korea Surfaced in 2000," *Washington Post*, October 19, 2002. Also see Mark Magnier and Sonni Efron, "E. Asian Strategic Balance Remains," *Los Angeles Times*, October 19, 2002.

ety about a potential nuclear crisis stimulated by President Bush's "axis of evil" remark, as well as by his subsequent decision in late March not to certify North Korea's compliance with the Agreed Framework. It also produced a commitment by Kim Jong Il to resume inter-Korean cooperation—including restarting reunions of separated families, rescheduling economic talks, and reopening talks between military authorities—as well as a new agreement to develop a second rail link between the two Koreas along the east coast. All this helped smooth U.S.-ROK relations and defuse accusations by radicals and others in South Korea of a nefarious U.S. desire to prevent inter-Korean reconciliation.

What it did not do was reform North Korea's behavior. Over the next three months, North Korea implemented only one of the commitments it made to Ambassador Lim in early April: another (fourth) round of family reunions at the end of that month. Even this took place only after South Korea agreed to hold the reunion at Mt. Kumgang in the North, rather than in each other's capitals as had previously been the practice. Aside from this singular event, no official inter-Korean activities took place, ostensibly because of North Korean unhappiness with the South Korean foreign minister.[58]

Instead of forming a new approach, North Korea reverted to form. It withdrew from inter-Korean economic talks—which would have been the first such talks in nearly a year and a half—one day before they were to take place (May 7–10). It canceled a North Korean tour of South Korean factories scheduled for late May. It also backed out of an agreement it made with a group of South Korean welfare foundation members to hold a joint church service with North Korean believers in Pyongyang, prohibiting the members from leaving their hotel unless they agreed to attend a politically sensitive North Ko-

---

[58]In mid-April Foreign Minister Choi Sung Hong was quoted as saying that "sometimes carrying a big stick works" in dealing with North Korea. This remark infuriated North Korea, which saw Choi as supporting Washington's "hard-line" policy, and it abruptly suspended all dialogue several weeks later. This, in turn, exasperated South Korea. For the foreign minister's quote, see Fred Hiatt, "N. Korea: What a Big Stick Can Do," *Washington Post*, April 23, 2002. On the exasperation in South Korea, see Barbara Demick, "N. Korea Cancels Planned Meeting," *Los Angeles Times*, May 7, 2002.

rean festival.[59] North Korea also ignored both its promise of inter-Korean military talks—despite a South Korean decision in May to indefinitely postpone publication of its annual Defense White Paper so as not to offend North Korean sensitivities—and its offer to open a second rail link between the two Koreas. Press reports that Kim Jong Il had told South Korean National Assemblywoman Park Geun-hye during her visit to Pyongyang in mid-May that he would honor both his promise to visit Seoul and a number of other commitments appeared, a month later, to be similarly unfounded.[60]

Not surprisingly, much of the energy in the public debate dissipated. The issues remained, as did the fundamental divisions. But with so little happening in North-South relations, they were largely dormant. Instead, South Koreans increasingly turned their attention to other issues: the economic situation, social—especially educational but also medical care—reform, and a seemingly endless series of political scandals. The latter, which led to the arrest of two of President Kim's sons and a decision by the president in May to formally quit the MDP in an effort to distance his party from the escalating scandals, particularly absorbed South Koreans.[61] The cumulative effect of political scandal and disenchantment with the government's North Korea and domestic policies was significant. In the June 13 local elections, the opposition GNP won a landslide victory, taking 11 of the 16 provincial governor and mayor contests and sweeping most of the 232 races for heads of small cities, counties, and district wards.[62]

---

[59]The South Korean government had previously prohibited the group from attending the festival. Lee Dong-hyun, "Prayers, Hymns Sound in Pyongyang," *JoongAng Ilbo*, June 20, 2002.

[60]As the daughter of former South Korean President Park Chung Hee, Park presented herself as having something unique to share with the son of North Korea's long-time leader, Kim Il Sung. As someone who had recently bolted the GNP to explore forming her own party and running for president herself, she sought to use her North Korea visit to strengthen her domestic political standing. The decision by the government to allow her to visit North Korea was widely interpreted as designed to damage the GNP in the run-up to the election.

[61]Kim had previously resigned his position as head of the ruling party in a similar effort. Joohee Cho, "S. Korean President Resigns from Party," *Washington Post*, May 7, 2002.

[62]Neighboring Cheju-do was the only province outside President Kim's home province to support the ruling party's candidate. "The People's Choice," *KOREA Now*, June 15, 2002.

Voter disapproval of government conduct, however, did not mean voter preoccupation with Pyongyang. As World Cup fever swept the country in the second half of June, the general sense was that most South Koreans had stopped thinking about the North altogether.

North Korea's unprovoked firing on and sinking of a ROK Navy patrol boat on June 29 changed the picture. This incident—coming the day before the closing ceremony of the World Cup while South Koreans were basking in the extraordinary performance of their team and country—left five South Korean sailors dead and many others injured. It also left the sunshine policy in tatters. Critics launched blistering attacks on the government for its alleged negligence, naiveté, and "continuous giveaway" in the face of North Korean provocations.[63] Supporters either switched or withheld support, seeing both North Korea's action and the government's meek response as indefensible.[64] Even the Ministry of Defense got into the act, criticizing the government for its passivity and calling for revision of the military "rules of engagement" to permit more aggressive action in the future. Most citizens seethed with anger toward North Korea. Public opinion as a whole toughened up notably.[65] For its part, the United States resisted pressure from the ROK government to continue with its plan to send a high-level U.S. official to Pyongyang to discuss resumption of U.S.-DPRK dialogue and postponed the plan in July. All this left the ROK government with not much choice but to demand an apology from Pyongyang and try to preserve the existing North-South agreements.

---

[63]Chun Young-gi, "Politicians Exchange Fire over Naval Battle," *JoongAng Ilbo*, July 2, 2002.

[64]For a good example, see Kwon Young-bin, "Sunshine Policy is No End in Itself," *JoongAng Ilbo*, July 8, 2002. Kwon is the editorial page editor of the *JoongAng Ilbo* and someone who, as a long-time supporter of the sunshine policy, worked hard to maintain balance in the newspaper's editorial comments over the years on the government's policies. Other representative reactions include: Paik Jin-hyun, "Cockeyed Optimism Hurts Seoul," *JoongAng Ilbo*, July 8, 2002; Lee Chung-min, "Weapons Useless Without the Will," *JoongAng Ilbo*, July 9, 2002; and Song Chin-hyok, "No Sunshine on a One-way Street," *JoongAng Ilbo*, July 11, 2002.

[65]According to one Gallup Korea/*Chosun Ilbo* poll taken a week after the naval incident, for example, some 70 percent of the respondents saw the clash as a premeditated provocation. A total of 75 percent said the sunshine policy should either be complemented with a tougher security stance (59.3 percent) or replaced altogether (15.8 percent). *Chosun Ilbo*, July 8, 2002.

There things might have stood had North Korea not abruptly reversed direction one month later. On July 25, the regime expressed "regret" for the "accidental" naval incident and proposed talks to discuss a resumption of inter-Korean dialogue.[66] With only four and a half months remaining before South Korea's next presidential election, President Kim chose to interpret the statement of "regret" as an "apology" and accepted the North Korean offer. This led to a flurry of activity unrivaled since the months immediately following the June 2000 North-South summit.

Some of this activity marked the resumption of endeavors long in train but long moribund or suspended. The seventh round of inter-ministerial talks, for example, was finally held in mid-August (after a delay of over nine months) and produced agreement to hold another round of family reunions and an array of additional meetings.[67] Similarly, the second South-North economic talks were held at the end of August (for the first time since December 2000) and resulted in an agreement to open two rail links across the demilitarized zone, restart talks on the Kaesong industrial complex, and pursue a series of additional cooperative activities and meetings.[68] Other activities in September—such as a friendly North-South soccer match, North Korean participation in the Asian Games in South Korea, and an agreement signed between the two sides' military authorities to avoid clashes while work was done to reconnect the cross-border rail links—were unprecedented.

The fact that all this activity occurred amid signs of incipient but potentially significant internal North Korean reforms stimulated much discussion of whether this time North Korea might actually be serious about changing its traditional orientation.[69] Japanese Prime

---

[66]For details, see Lee Young-jong, "North 'Regrets' Battle, Seeks Talks," *JoongAng Ilbo*, July 25, 2002; and Christopher Torchia, "N. Korea Says It Regrets Clash With South, Proposes Talks," *Washington Post*, July 26, 2002.

[67]ROK Ministry of Unification, "Joint Press Statement of the 7th Inter-Korean Ministerial Talks," *Korean Unification Bulletin*, No. 46, August 2002, pp. 1–2.

[68]ROK Ministry of Unification, "Inter-Korean Economic Cooperation Promotion Committee holds the Second Meeting," and "Agreement at the Second Inter-Korean Economic Cooperation Promotion Committee," ibid., pp. 3–4.

[69]Aidan Foster-Carter, "No Turning Back?" *Comparative Connections*, 3rd Quarter 2002. For short accounts of the North Korean reforms, see James A. Foley, "Pyongyang Introduces Market Reforms," *Jane's Intelligence Review*, September 1, 2002; Doug

Minister Koizumi's surprise visit to Pyongyang in mid-September, which resulted in unexpected progress on long-standing bilateral issues, reinforced the sense of change and heartened ROK government supporters.[70] To be sure, the North Korean turnaround came too late to help President Kim politically. In the August by-elections for the National Assembly, the opposition GNP won another landslide victory, taking 11 of the 13 vacant seats being contested. This gave the GNP a majority of 139 seats in the assembly and the power to push bills through the legislature unilaterally.[71] Still, supporters of the sunshine policy took the renewed activity as confirmation of the wisdom and efficacy of the government's patient, consistent approach toward North Korea.

South Korean critics and opponents of the sunshine policy, on the other hand, found much missing. There was no actual "apology" for North Korea's intentional and unprovoked sinking of the South Korean naval vessel, many charged, only a statement of "regret" for an "accidental" incident. There was no sign of North Korean willingness to begin talks on pressing military issues. And there was no agreement on a Kim Jong Il visit to Seoul. Many of the agreed-upon measures, moreover, were either indefinite (e.g., a certain meeting will be held "at an early date") or left to be decided later. Other aspects of the flurry of activity—ranging from absence of attention to the plight of North Korean refugees to the enormous costs associated with rebuilding the North's worn out rail system—reminded many South Korean critics of what they do not like about the sunshine policy. In the process, the spate of activity revived debate again over the government's approach toward North Korea.

Not surprisingly, Prime Minister Koizumi's visit to Pyongyang in mid-September contributed to the revival. Many South Koreans compared the results of his visit to that of President Kim in 2000 and

---

Struck, "A Taste of Capitalism in North Korea," *Washington Post*, September 13, 2002; Chang-hyun Jung and Yong-soo Jeong, "Next Step for North's Economy: Foreign Direct Investment," *JoongAng Ilbo*, September 16, 2002; and Marcus Noland, "Trainspotting in North Korea," *Far Eastern Economic Review*, October 24, 2002.

[70]For a short description of the Koizumi visit, see Howard French, "North Koreans Sign Agreement with Japanese," *The New York Times*, September 18, 2002.

[71]Kim Hyung-jin, "Following Another Election Triumph, GNP Set to Flex Parliamentary Muscles," *Korea Herald*, August 10, 2002.

found the latter lacking. Conservatives in particular were enraged at Koizumi's success in gaining information about the relative handful of Japanese abducted by North Korea over the years, whereas President Kim had never even raised the issue of the vastly larger number of South Koreans seized by Pyongyang and taken to North Korea.[72] Subsequent allegations by South Korean opposition politicians that President Kim had secretly funneled some $400 million to the North shortly before and after the June 2000 summit, while denied by the Blue House, intensified South Korea's political divisions.[73]

Still, the debate might have attenuated at this point had North Korea continued to provide evidence of significant, substantive change and a genuine willingness to live in peace with South Korea.[74] As it happens, the warmth that had appeared so suddenly in inter-Korean relations turned out to be a false spring. North Korea's admission to U.S. Assistant Secretary of State James Kelly in early October (made public two weeks later) that it has been pursuing a covert nuclear weapons program for years in violation of multiple international, inter-Korean, and U.S.-DPRK agreements startled the world and rattled inter-Korean relations.[75] Its defiant insistence that it is "entitled to possess not only nuclear weapons but any type of weapon more

---

[72]Officially the government says North Korea has abducted nearly 3,800 South Koreans since the end of the Korean War, although others place the total in the tens of thousands. Aidan Foster-Carter, "No Turning Back?" op. cit., 2002.

[73]For an English account, see Andrew Ward, "S. Korea 'Bribed North to Improve Relations,'" *Financial Times*, October 1, 2002.

[74]Barbara Demick, "North Korea's Goodwill Gestures Spark Debate," *Los Angeles Times*, September 19, 2002.

[75]Peter Slevin and Karen DeYoung, "N. Korea Admits Having Secret Nuclear Arms—Stunned U.S. Ponders Next Steps," *Washington Post*, October 17, 2002. Kelly subsequently said he told the North Koreans that the U.S. had been prepared to present a "bold approach to improve bilateral relations"—one that would involve "significant economic and diplomatic steps to improve the lives of the North Korean people"—if North Korea "dramatically altered its behavior" on a range of issues of concern to the United States. He added, however, that information indicating that North Korea is conducting a program to enrich uranium for nuclear weapons in violation of its international commitments made such an approach impossible. Kelly was surprised when, after initial denials, the North Koreans not only "flatly acknowledged that they have such a program" but also declared that they considered the Agreed Framework "nullified." For the text of Kelly's statement, see "Statement by Assistant Secretary of State for East Asian and Pacific Affairs James A. Kelly," October 19, 2002. A copy provided by the American Embassy Information Resource Center is available at http://usembassy.state.gov/seoul/wwwh43cv.html.

powerful than that" shook the foundation on which not only South Korean but all international efforts to improve relations with North Korea had been predicated—namely, a good faith North Korean effort to comply with its nonproliferation commitments.[76]   With this admission, the sun set on the sunshine policy. And winter returned with a vengeance.

---

[76]The reference to weapons "more powerful" than nuclear weapons presumably alludes to biological weapons, although North Korea also has a large stock of chemical weapons available for use. For excerpts from the text of North Korea's official press release, see "North Korea's Response," *The New York Times*, October 26, 2002.

Chapter Seven

CONCLUSIONS AND IMPLICATIONS

South Korea's engagement policy is the result of a long, evolutionary process. Its pursuit under President Kim, however, has not been a simple continuation of previous policy. Indeed, in important respects it represents a significant departure, particularly in the substitution of "reconciliation" for "unification" as the policy's operative objective, the de facto jettisoning of reciprocity as a central policy component, and the priority given to helping North Korea. The emphasis given to sustaining political dialogue, the trust placed in Kim Jong Il as a partner for peace, and the tendency in practice to overlook or subordinate important security issues are other critical differences with preceding governments.

Much of the debate over the government's policy is a product of differences among South Koreans over these policy departures. Although there certainly are people in South Korea who oppose dealings with North Korea altogether, the main debate has been over the way in which engagement has been practiced rather than over engagement per se. Extensive questioning of many of the assumptions underlying the government's approach—such as that major internal changes can be produced in the North simply by renouncing "absorption" or providing "assurances" of the regime's survival—broaden the debate's scope. So too does similar questioning of the manner in which policy has been formulated and implemented.

To be sure, partisan politics are clearly a component of the debate. At its core, however, are some big questions:

- What should be the aim of any effort to achieve greater association with North Korea—"reconciliation" on the basis of Korea
  being "one people" or "unification" by extending South Korea's
  democratic, free-market system to the North?

- What role should reciprocity play in this effort?

- What should be the nature and scale of South Korean assistance
  to North Korea?

- How should political efforts to engage North Korea be balanced
  against South Korea's security and other important interests?

- How should the effectiveness of the government's policies be
  evaluated?

What has made the debate so intense is the way in which it has re-
opened deeper, long-standing fissures within South Korean society.
These fissures divide South Koreans sharply along political, regional,
and ideological lines. The latter in particular have contributed to
polarizing the debate and undermining public consensus behind the
government's policies. In the process, they have made the sunshine
policy the core issue in a much larger political and ideological struggle.

How all this happened is itself a matter of debate. One view, widely
held among ROK government supporters, intellectuals, and progressive groups today, identifies the United States as the principal cause
of the difficulties facing the sunshine policy. According to those who
hold this view, the new "hard-line" policy of the Bush administration
and distrust expressed toward Kim Jong Il alarmed and offended
North Korea, causing it to back off from dialogue with both South
Korea and the United States. This in turn stimulated both the opposition parties—who allegedly do not want to see progress in
North-South relations anyway because the MDP would be the chief
beneficiary—and other conservative groups with their own "anti-
Communist" agendas to do everything they could to prevent the Kim
administration from achieving its objectives. Mounting domestic
scandals, vigorously pursued by these same conservative forces, facilitated this effort and eroded over time the administration's moral
authority and political standing. U.S. policies contributed indirectly
to this, those with this view argue, by seriously "embarrassing" the
South Korean president and undermining his position with both

North Korea and the South Korean public. From this perspective, the United States ruined the "golden opportunity" created by the Clinton administration in its last three months in office and—only a few months after the historic summit—cut off the most promising prospects for North-South reconciliation since the two Koreas were established.

Other people stress the role of North Korea. According to them, the North squandered valuable time in not responding to the administration's entreaties. When it did finally respond, it failed to honor most of its commitments. It also gave the impression that it was toying with the ROK government, repeatedly canceling meetings at the last minute without any explanation, refusing to discuss previously agreed-upon matters, and suspending dialogue altogether for protracted periods. The North Koreans also passed up countless opportunities to support those in the ROK government who argued that Kim Jong Il is a genuine partner for peace worthy of assistance. The one time Pyongyang did try to be helpful—offering to restart inter-Korean ministerial talks on the eve of the National Assembly no-confidence vote on Lim Dong-Won—the attempt backfired. The offer, which most South Koreans saw as a transparent effort to influence the outcome of the assembly vote, set off a firestorm of criticism in South Korea. Meanwhile, the North significantly stepped up its efforts to exploit the divisions in South Korean society. It maintained its military buildup and other threatening behavior. It also repeatedly did things (naval incidents, the Russia–North Korea joint communiqué, etc.) that undermined Kim Dae Jung's credibility and political standing with the South Korean public. The best policies in the world, those with this view maintain, could not succeed in the face of this kind of behavior.

There is some merit in each of these interpretations. To be sure, emphasis on the importance of the Bush administration's "hard line" overlooks the fundamental continuity in U.S. policies. The administration's emphasis on the importance of North-South reconciliation, repeated public endorsements of the South Korean government's engagement policy, and stress on President Kim's leading role in resolving inter-Korean issues are all aspects of previous U.S. policy that survived the transition. So too are the Bush administration's pledge to adhere to the Agreed Framework; repeated calls for a serious, unconditional dialogue with North Korea; and offers of significant steps toward normal relations in exchange for comparable steps by Pyong-yang to address priority issues on the U.S. agenda. Other examples are the Bush administration's decision to have President Kim be the first Asian visitor invited to the White House and its active efforts to revitalize U.S.-ROK and U.S.-ROK-Japan consultation mechanisms. Emphasis on the Bush administration's allegedly "hard line" both overlooks the fundamental continuity in U.S. policy and understates the lengths to which the administration has gone to be supportive of what it considers a valued ally.

Still, the advent of the Bush administration gave Pyongyang yet an-other pretext for breaking off dialogue with South Korea, and the more distrustful stance taken by Washington—as filtered through a South Korean media explicitly focused on furthering its own inter-ests—bolstered those in the ROK who shared similar views. As the aftermath of September 11 combined with growing evidence of a continuing North Korean nuclear weapons program, a perceived gap developed between U.S. priorities and those of the South Korean government. This was a potential vulnerability President Kim's domestic opponents were more than eager to exploit—and which his supporters actively countered. To this extent, the United States probably did reinforce the divisions already existing in South Korea and contribute indirectly to the decline in public support for the sunshine policy.

In the case of North Korea, the contributions were undeniable. Put simply, Pyongyang was its own worst enemy. Whatever its goals or intentions, its conduct communicated a fundamental unwillingness to either come to terms with South Korea or abide by international norms and practices. This, together with its demonstrative effort to inflame social tensions in the South, undermined the willingness of most South Koreans to explain away North Korean behavior. It also undermined several key ROK government arguments: that Kim Jong Il could be trusted, that the regime was no longer a threat, and that the sunshine policy was effective in both enhancing South Korea's security and producing broader change in Pyongyang. In this sense, North Korea's contributions to the struggle in South Korean politics over North-South issues and the loss of support for the government's policies were both real and direct. Its admission of a continuing covert program to develop nuclear weapons probably by itself sealed the fate of the sunshine policy.

Whatever the importance of these two external actors, the policy's prospects have been heavily shaped by South Korea's own *internal* dynamics. These played a major role in reopening the fissures in South Korean society and polarizing public opinion. Here, the list of contributing factors is long:

- *The government's minority status:* President Kim was elected with a plurality of some 300,000 votes. Even then he was elected only by forming a strange coalition—in political and policy terms—with Kim Jong-pil's ULD. His own party, moreover, was a distinct minority within the National Assembly. This was a major constraining factor from the beginning, both within the government and between the government and National Assembly. The logic of the situation suggested the need for the president to broaden his base of support in order to build greater consensus behind his policies. Although he moved cautiously in the early period of his administration, on the whole this was not his general inclination. Instead, he used his sunshine policy overtly and intentionally to improve both his personal political position and his party's electoral prospects. This was neither unique for a politician nor unreasonable given the president's particular situation. But it helped rile the political opposition, politicize what had generally been considered a nonpartisan issue, and heighten the perceived stakes in domestic political terms. As reflected in the administration's inability to secure support for electricity assistance to the North or funding for other planned government initiatives, it also exacerbated the task of gaining legislative approval for government policies. One by-product was an increased National Assembly role in and influence over government policy.

- *The role of reciprocity:* Reciprocity was important on its own terms of course. Support for government policies in any democratic society hinges ultimately on a public view that such policies are effective in advancing important national interests. Absent clear manifestations of North Korean reciprocity, the "payback" for South Korea's largesse became increasingly hard to demonstrate. This was particularly true in the context of continued North Korean military provocations. One effect was an administration tendency to oversell its policy successes, which over time corroded its credibility. The failure to insist on reciprocity was important in another respect as well: It magnified the effect of the ruling party's minority status. By not educating Kim Jong Il about the importance of public opinion in a democracy and insisting on specific reciprocal gestures for specific South Korean acts, President Kim denied himself an important tool for shaping public opinion. Many South Koreans believe he may also have oversold North Korean leaders on his ability to deliver on his promises, reinforcing Kim Jong Il's emphasis on relations with the United States and reluctance to develop a serious relationship with South Korea.

- *The approach to domestic critics*: The president's confidence and conviction were valuable in at least two ways. First, they provided a compass that kept policy focused despite many challenges. Second, they succored the administration in the face of severe domestic criticism. The downside was a certain hard-headedness that closed the policymaking process to all but the closest of the president's aids and blinded the administration to the dangers of mounting domestic opposition. Many South Koreans insist that the administration exacerbated its difficulties further by how it chose to deal with its critics. Although there was not much actual criticism of the sunshine policy in the early period, the administration was harshly critical of those who did express doubts or reservations almost from the beginning. Indeed, the rhetoric used was often so harsh—accusing those who criticized the policy of being "anti-unification" and, in effect, unpatriotic—that it validated long-standing suspicions among South Korean conservatives about the president's ideological propensities and intentions. This had a predictable effect: While it heartened the radical left and secured its allegiance, it alienated many more in the middle of the political spectrum and narrowed the potential base for national consensus. Informed South Koreans suggest that the president's rigidity and intolerance grew worse over time. Although he was always knowledgeable about the domestic situation, according to these observers, he simply stopped listening.

- *The war with the press*: The administration's attack on the media under the rubric of "reforming" the press is widely seen as at least partly a manifestation of this intolerance for domestic criticism. The attack was even more consequential than the administration's harsh rhetoric, however, in consolidating opposition to the sunshine policy. Admittedly, the administration faced certain problems in dealing with the press that were beyond its control: Most of the dominant, mainstream press is very conservative in its political orientations, and most have long held attitudes toward President Kim that range somewhere between distrust and antipathy. Still, the administration's effort to silence the press and *force* it to adopt reforms dictated by the government was more than simply anomalous, given the president's reputation as a champion of democracy and human rights. It was also counterproductive. The attack severely alienated the mainstream press and stimulated a de facto alliance between it and the opposition parties to prevent the government from achieving its objectives. The attack also exacerbated the administration's difficulty in mobilizing public support for the steps it wanted to take with North Korea, since it could enlist only the leftist media in efforts to rally support for its policies. In a populace as inherently conservative as that of South Korea, a battle between the overwhelmingly dominant *Chosun Ilbo* and the more fringe *Hankyoreh Sinmun* was one the government was destined to lose.

- *The lack of trust and willingness to compromise*: These cultural characteristics have historically bedeviled Korean politics, contributing among other things to political rigidity and a "winner-takes-all" orientation. South Korea's short experience with democratization has provided little time for alternative approaches to be developed. This lack affected the political dynamics at virtually all levels. Within the ruling coalition, the MDP and ULD each used the other to maximize its own political position without reaching a viable compromise on their very different views about policy toward North Korea. Similarly, the opposition parties—each containing both conservative and progressive National Assemblymen—had to deal with their own internal confrontations. This made it difficult to even reach intra-party accord, let alone adopt a more accommodating stance vis-à-vis the ruling coalition. Attempts by the government to exploit these internal confrontations intensified the distrust between the ruling and opposition camps and further fueled the opposition's unwillingness to compromise.

Other internal factors contributing to the evolution of events could easily be identified. The extreme personalization of policy, for example, saddled the effort to engage North Korea with all of the president's personal baggage. The administration's reluctance to acknowledge the underlying continuity in South Korean policies removed an important shield against both North Korean manipulation and domestic partisan attack. And the government's refusal to convey the actual state of the North-South relationship to the public—its tendency to emphasize only what North Korea had "said" it would do rather than what it actually wound up doing—generated continual disappointment and public cynicism. More broadly, the administration's emphasis on "trusting" the North in the absence of a widely apparent basis for this trust, and its periodic efforts to palliate the North through policy and personnel changes, created an impression of governmental naiveté and weakness. North Korea's behavior made it easy for critics to exploit this impression. These factors combined to dissipate support for the government's engagement efforts.

Ultimately, however, the story of how consensus evaporated so quickly is less about particular governmental "mistakes" than about the broader interactions among politicians, press, and public opinion, with civic groups on both sides of an increasingly polarized citizenry serving as flag bearers in a larger political and ideological struggle. This struggle reflects both the continued hold of old, unresolved issues and the impact of South Korea's new process of democratization. It also illustrates how, after decades of repressive, authoritarian rule, democracy has become a permanent feature of the South Korean landscape.

The bad news for government supporters is that the sunshine policy has been dealt a seemingly fatal blow. Even before the revelations concerning North Korea's clandestine uranium enrichment effort, the policy was wrapped up in ideological, regional, and partisan bickering. The obstacles to unwrapping the policy, moreover, were substantial. The government lacked a majority in the National Assembly. Its popularity was limited mostly to President Kim's own home region. And public confidence was at an all-time low. While the spurt of activity in August and September 2002 stimulated hopes among sunshine policy supporters that the North had turned decisively toward genuine reconciliation, the regime's admission in October that it is pursuing a secret nuclear weapons program confirmed the worst fears of the policy's opponents.

North Korea's startling admission had three immediate effects: It stimulated widespread confusion about North Korean motives; it strengthened those who had long argued the regime cannot be trusted; and it further undermined public confidence in the administration's handling of North-South relations. As a practical political matter, the admission preempted all other issues on the policy agenda, while shattering what little was left of Pyongyang's credibility as a negotiating partner. Until and unless the nuclear issue is resolved, the sun is not likely to shine again on North Korea.

Even in the unlikely event the nuclear issue were resolved quickly, it would be very difficult for the administration to move far forward in inter-Korean relations. This is not necessarily a statement about either the intentions or abilities of the current administration. The truth is that it would be hard for any government to pursue an effective engagement policy today. The bedrock requirement for any such policy is a strong national consensus. Achieving such a consensus, in turn, requires many things: a favorable international environment, a responsive North Korean partner, a perceived balance between South Korean initiatives and North Korean reciprocity, a supportive economy, and public trust. None of these exist today.

In the short term, therefore, advances in North-South relations will be put on ice. The administration will try to maintain the basic framework of its policies—emphasizing continued humanitarian assistance and direct North-South contact—while the nuclear issue is adjudicated. It also will try to preserve the Agreed Framework and as many of the existing North-South agreements as possible. But the task of building a new approach toward inter-Korean relations will fall to President Kim's successor.

North Korea, as always, remains a wild card. Kim Jong Il has demonstrated a capacity for bold, unexpected actions. He could pull a "November surprise" and visit Seoul or make some other grand, enticing gesture. Although the odds are small, were this to happen it would have an explosive effect on both politics and public debate inside South Korea. Most South Korean voters would see such a move as a blatant attempt to influence the outcome of the presidential election.

Quite apart from the nuclear issue, the internal dynamics of the debate over the sunshine policy are likely to have several short-term implications. First, it is likely that South Korea will continue to be weighed down by history. The intensity of feelings toward President Kim alone will keep the country mired in the past, as will recriminations and debate over his legacy. This could impede timely South Korean responses to international terrorism and other "new era" issues.

Second, the political situation is likely to get worse before it gets better. Politically, much of President Kim's desire to perpetuate his record is tied up with the outcome of the December election. Any hopes of seeing his policies institutionalized hinge on his party's electoral success. Moreover, the personal stakes could not be higher. If the MDP loses the election, there could well be an investigation of the president similar to the one he himself conducted of his predecessor, Kim Young Sam. In the former case, the goal was to politically destroy not just the ex-president but all those around him. As a practical matter, therefore, nearly everything the government does in its remaining months will be geared to winning the election. The political opposition, in turn, will do everything it can to besmirch the government's image and exploit the divisions within the MDP between supporters and opponents of its designated candidate, Roh Moo Hyun. Since historically the key to winning elections in South Korea has been to find ways to split the opposition, politics are likely to get quite nasty.

Third, the tendency some South Koreans have to blame the United States for particular problems will likely persist, if not increase further. This is particularly true of Kim Dae Jung's political supporters, whose close personal identification with the president almost necessitates a search for scapegoats in the event of policy disappointments. A major downturn in North-South relations will likely be added to the laundry list of issues these groups hold against the United States—a development North Korea may have anticipated in openly acknowledging its clandestine nuclear weapons program but, in any event, one it is certain to actively exploit.

Over the long term, the implications of the public debate are more encouraging. Put simply, democratization is working. Civilian government is permanently in place. The military has been returned to the barracks. And influential institutions—the press, the National Assembly, academia, church and civic organizations—have taken root to inform public policy and check the arbitrary use of executive power. While the president continues to weigh heavily in South Korean politics and policy, the highly educated, middle-class electorate has become a real factor affecting his or her prospects for success. As a result, public opinion now matters. The public debate over policy toward the North in this sense is healthy. It brings long-suppressed issues out into the open and allows the sharply divergent views and approaches of South Korean citizens to be aired and adjudicated. Greater consensus—and a broader, steadier center—will undoubtedly emerge over time. The long-term prospect, therefore, is for South Korea to become a more stable and secure democracy.

Getting from here to there, however, will itself take time. Whoever is elected in December, the next period will constitute a transition from the era of the three Kims to a new era in South Korean politics. In any such transition period, the fundamental fault lines in society—especially ideological divisions rooted in long-standing, unresolved historical issues—cannot be expected to end overnight. South Korea is no exception. Even a sweeping GNP victory in December will not end these underlying divisions. This means that for some time to come South Korean politics will remain polarized, personalized, and raw.

The likely effects of the election on policies toward the North are more uncertain. Contrary to the conventional wisdom suggesting that basic South Korean policies will continue no matter who wins the election, the last decade demonstrates that leadership makes a difference. If the GNP wins the election, it is likely that South Korea will adopt a significantly tougher stance—more in line with the "tough love" school identified in Chapter Four—toward North Korea. This would entail greater emphasis on reciprocity, verifiable threat reduction, and South Korea's alliance with the United States. It also would involve renewed stress on the ROK's traditional approach toward unification. This would focus more on "peaceful coexistence" than on "reconciliation" as the operative goal of South Korea's policy and give higher priority to strengthening South Korean military and economic capability as the means for achieving its long-term goal of unification on South Korean terms. A GNP government would probably seek to maintain some kind of engagement with North Korea, but it is likely to give greater emphasis to South Korea's security interests as it pursues resolution of the nuclear issue and any resumed North-South dialogue.

If the MDP or some successor party wins, the government would likely maintain the essence of the sunshine policy. Although some effort may be made to distance the new president personally from his predecessor, an MDP government would probably continue to seek inter-Korean "reconciliation." It also would try to protect North-South political interactions by emphasizing the need to resolve the nuclear issue "peacefully through dialogue." A Roh Moo Hyun government might even try to facilitate resolution of the nuclear issue by offering North Korea increased economic assistance or other inducements. Such efforts could increase strains between South Korea and the United States, particularly in the new administration's early, "learning curve" period. Even a Roh Moo Hyun government, however, would have to adapt its stance to the new reality caused by North Korea's defiant acknowledgment of continuing efforts to develop weapons of mass destruction. Implementation of the North-South denuclearization agreements and North Korea's other international nonnuclear commitments would likely remain a key South Korean demand and impediment to expanded North-South relations.

Whatever the outcome of the elections, the South Korean debate over policies toward the North will present the United States with both a challenge and an opportunity. On the one hand, few South Koreans are ready to trade engagement for confrontation. Even fewer want war. This fear of war transcends both party affiliation and ideological predisposition. While critics of the sunshine policy want to see significant changes in South Korea's approach toward the North, most also want to see continued progress toward tension reduction and peaceful coexistence. Avoiding the danger of being seen as an obstacle to peaceful coexistence between the two Koreas, while resolving the WMD issue and pursuing its larger strategic interests, will be a major challenge for U.S. policy throughout the coming period.

On the other hand, most South Koreans have lost patience with North Korea. While they tend to see North Korea's actions primarily as defensive measures to ensure its own survival, they recognize such actions as genuine threats to ROK security. Many also share the view that such continuing bad behavior should not be rewarded. By exposing its mendacity and malevolence, moreover, North Korea's admission of an ongoing WMD program reinforced the arguments of sunshine policy opponents that all agreements with Pyongyang must be verifiable and reciprocal. It also gave greater credence to the long-standing distrust expressed by U.S. officials. As the United States pursues resolution of the nuclear and other outstanding issues with North Korea, it has the opportunity to help establish a basis for greater consensus within South Korea on an appropriate "post-sunshine" policy toward North Korea and greater harmony in U.S. and ROK approaches.

How the North Korean WMD issue is resolved is thus critical. The debate in South Korea over the government's policy toward North Korea did not begin with Pyongyang's admission that it has been pursuing a secret nuclear weapons program in violation of multiple international and North-South agreements. But the debate's evolution will be an important determinant of how the South Korean and broader international response to this latest North Korean challenge ultimately ends. The debate and evolution of North-South relations will be major drivers of Korea's future more broadly and help determine security prospects throughout the Asia-Pacific region. Rarely has attention to internal developments in South Korea been more needed.